A PHILOSOPHY OF LONELINESS

A Philosophy of Loneliness

Lars Svendsen

REAKTION BOOKS

For Siri, Iben and Luna

Published by Reaktion Books Ltd
Unit 32, Waterside
44–48 Wharf Road
London N1 7UX, UK
www.reaktionbooks.co.uk

First published in English 2017, reprinted 2017
English-language translation © Reaktion Books 2017
English translation by Kerri Pierce

This book was first published in 2015 by Universitetsforlaget, Oslo
under the title *Ensomhetens Filosofi* by Lars Fr. H. Svendsen
Copyright © Universitetsforlaget 2015

This translation has been published with
the financial support of NORLA

Printed and bound in Great Britain
by Bell & Bain, Glasgow

A catalogue record for this book is available from
the British Library

ISBN 978 1 78023 747 3

Contents

Introduction

All is loneliness here for me
Loneliness here for me . . .
Loneliness

MOONDOG

Almost all I thought I knew about loneliness proved false. I thought more men than women were lonely, and that lonely people were more isolated than others. I assumed that the significant increase in the number of single dwellers would notably impact the number of lonely individuals. I thought social media generated more loneliness by displacing ordinary sociability. I also believed that loneliness, despite being a subjective phenomenon, could be better understood in the context of social surroundings than individual disposition. I believed the Scandinavian countries had higher degrees of loneliness, and that these numbers were increasing. Furthermore, I assumed that this increase was connected to late modern individualism, and that individualistic societies had higher rates of loneliness than collective societies.

Never have I worked with a subject that overturned to such an extent all the assumptions I brought to the table. And these preconceptions are quite widespread. Indeed, they can be considered the standard picture given to us by the mass media, where expressions such as 'loneliness epidemic' are common: at the moment I am writing this, a Google search of 'loneliness + epidemic' returns almost 400,000 hits. Yet when it comes to the problem of loneliness, the image created by all these assumptions is severely misleading. Indeed, it is difficult to find any other 'loneliness epidemic' than the one present in the mass media itself, in which use of the term 'loneliness' has been significantly rising for years. Loneliness is receiving steadily more attention, but that does not mean there is more of it out there.

Nonetheless, there is one assumption that rings true: loneliness can be a serious problem for those whom it affects. For many people, it significantly impacts their quality of life, not to mention their physical and mental health. However, loneliness is a difficult subject to address, because it is so laden with shame. At the same time, our best moments can come when we are alone. Solitude, as we tend to call it in this case, tells us something important about ourselves and our place in the world. This book is the result of my attempts to discover what exactly loneliness is, whom it affects, why the emotion of loneliness occurs, lingers and disappears, and how we can relate to loneliness as individuals and as a society.

A General Human Phenomenon

There is no need for me to describe the emotion of loneliness. You know it from your childhood, from a day when it seemed as though everyone else but you had a playmate; from an evening spent alone, though you would dearly have liked some company; from the party where you hardly knew a soul and stood surrounded by people busily engaged with each other; from the night you lay next to your girlfriend or boyfriend, well cognizant of the fact that the relationship was over; and from being in the empty apartment after they had left for the last time.

There is always a price to pay for love, and loneliness is part of that price. Anyone who cares about or loves another person will experience loneliness when that person is no longer there, when they have left you either physically or emotionally. Of course, you can always try to make yourself invulnerable by avoiding forming close ties to others, but the price for that is an even more substantial loneliness.

Loneliness detaches you from others in a meaningful way, and in that respect it also detaches your from yourself, from important sides of yourself that can only exist and develop through your ties to other people. Stendhal writes: 'Everything can be acquired in solitude, except character.'[1] It is, however, more than character that cannot be acquired when alone. Basically, you cannot become a human being in isolation. Your connections to other people and the experiences you have with them shape your very humanity. As C. S. Lewis writes, 'As soon as we are fully conscious we discover loneliness. We need others physically, emotionally, intellectually; we need them if we are to know anything, even ourselves.'[2] However, we have to take it one step further. We also need other people to need us.

You can be lonely in a crowd or at home, out in nature or in an empty church. Countless songs have been written about loneliness, but none seems to capture its essence quite as well as 'All is Loneliness', with its repetitive and crushing melancholy. The song was originally written by the blind and homeless New York artist Moondog (1916–1999). He wrote the song while sitting in a doorway in Manhattan – in the middle of one of the world's most densely populated cities. As Georg Simmel observes in his essay 'The Metropolis and Mental Life', there is scarcely any place one feels so lonely as in a metropolis.[3] He emphasizes that loneliness does not imply the lack of community, but rather an unfulfilled ideal of community.[4] If we were not social creatures, loneliness would not exist. It is precisely because we are social creatures that we find inhabiting a social space where we lack ties to anyone so lonely. Alexis de Tocqueville was making the same point as early as the 1930s, in his study of democracy in America.[5] In one letter he observes that solitude in a desert is less harsh than solitude among men.[6] The gloomy image of the big city is well illustrated by a cartoon from the *New Yorker* from 2004 showing a street vendor with a sign that says: 'Eye Contact, $1.00'. Loneliness certainly exists in large cities, but it is not only found there. Loneliness exists wherever people exist, and it does not seem to be any more prevalent in a metropolis than in smaller towns or rural areas.

Everyone is probably lonely from time to time. A person who has never felt lonely presumably suffers from some emotional lack or defect. The reason for this is simple. From the time they are very young, humans require a connection to others, and it is impossible for this need to be met at every single moment during a person's life. On the other hand, it must be conceded that a large percentage of respondents on surveys on the subject claim that they are 'never' lonely. I interpret this to mean that, typically speaking, they are not lonely, but that they certainly know the feeling, and that loneliness is a standing possibility in their lives.

In fact, many people claim that we are living today in the 'the age of loneliness',[7] that we do, in fact, have an 'epidemic of loneliness'[8] on our hands. Still, we have no reason to believe that loneliness is more widespread today than it was in earlier times. Indeed, there are epidemiological studies that provide a certain basis for evaluating the trend over the last few decades, and these generally suggest that loneliness is not any more widespread than it was previously. Furthermore, if we shift our context more towards a history of ideas, we do not find that the concept emerges at a particular point in time and quickly becomes prevalent, as is the case with 'boredom'.[9] Variations of the concept can be found circulating from Old Testament times up to today. The discussion surrounding loneliness has surged at certain times, for instance during the Enlightenment and Romantic eras, but unlike 'boredom' it is directly tied to social changes occurring in those times, since loneliness had long been established as a general human emotion. Nonetheless, the last three decades have seen an increase in loneliness studies, and even though increased awareness of a problem might give us reason to think its severity is also increasing, we have no basis for assuming that to be the case here.

Moreover, when I differentiate in this book between the lonely and the non-lonely, these idealizations can create the impression that individuals are so uniform that they can be divided into one group or the other, with a clear line drawn between them, whereas in reality we are talking about a continuum. General statements about loneliness must always be read with the idea in mind that enormous variation exists in both the causes and experiences of loneliness. Obviously, the emotion experienced by a bullying victim is primarily due to external causes, whereas the persistent loneliness of a person whose entire life has been spent surrounded by friends and a loving family must instead be sought in that individual's inner emotional and cognitive dispositions or in the development of them. General statements such as 'the lonely have a stronger tendency towards x', in which x indicates a cognitive, emotional or behavioural characteristic, underscore traits that are especially prevalent in the group 'the lonely', but there is significant variation within the group itself, and of course a given member of the group does not have to demonstrate that characteristic. It would certainly be preferable to be able to differentiate better, such that we could say that characteristic x is especially prevalent among those with loneliness type a, and not among those with loneliness type b, but there is simply not enough research to be able to do this to a meaningful extent.

Generally, people report that time spent together with others is more satisfying than time spent alone,[10] but there are significant individual variations. Simply being alone is in essence neither positive nor negative. Everything depends on how you are alone. To be alone – all-one, where I alone am all – is to be in a situation where we have some of our best and some of our worst moments. It is the positive variant that E. M. Cioran describes when he writes: 'At this moment, I am alone. What more can I want? A more intense happiness does not exist. Yes: that of hearing, by dint of silence, my solitude enlarge.'[11] The negative extreme, on the other hand, is chronicled in Sartre's *Nausea*, where we find:

> I felt myself in a solitude so frightful that I contemplated suicide. What held me back was the idea that no one, absolutely no one, would be moved by my death, that I would be even more alone in death than in life.[12]

Sartre's Roquentin is hardly alone in expressing such despair. Mark Twain's Huckleberry Finn, J. D. Salinger's Holden Caulfield and countless other novelistic protagonists complain of being so alone they wish they could die. Others, however, recognize the pain implicit in loneliness, but nonetheless believe that the experience is essential for personal growth. This is why Rainer Maria Rilke writes: 'love your solitude and bear the pain which it has caused you with fair-sounding lament.'[13]

Human life is such that there is no guarantee that our need for connection will be satisfied. Some people are infrequently lonely, some almost never, while others are lonely most of the time. Loneliness can strike in the midst of everyday life or in a serious life crisis. We all know the emotion, yet we do not all experience it in the same way. Only among a minority is loneliness sustained as a serious problem over a long duration. Indeed, some people experience it in so many different situations and so frequently that their loneliness must be considered chronic. Periodic loneliness, on the other hand, while no doubt uncomfortable or painful, is also manageable. Chronic loneliness, however, is a condition that threatens to undermine a person's entire existence.

One example of this kind of loneliness from the world of film is Travis Bickle, the protagonist in Martin Scorsese's *Taxi Driver*. As he says: 'Loneliness has followed me my whole life, everywhere. In bars, in cars, sidewalks, stores, everywhere. There's no escape. I'm God's lonely man.' (Incidentally, that last phrase was taken by screenplay writer Paul Schrader from Thomas Wolfe's famous essay of the same title.) In this context, it is also worth mentioning that Adam's loneliness is the first thing God does not consider favourable in his Creation: 'And the Lord God said, "It is not good that the man should be alone."'[14] This theme often appears in biblical texts. In Psalms, David complains that no one is concerned for him;[15] Ecclesiastes emphasizes how much harder life is for the lonely.[16] And hardly anyone has been lonelier than Job, although Christ on the cross must have been.

We all have an inherent duplicity or antagonism that draws us towards others because we need them, and also pushes us away because we need distance, need to be left alone. Immanuel Kant formulates this nicely in his expression 'unsocial sociability'.[17] Both poles of this antagonism contain loneliness, though one is experienced negatively and the other positively. This duality further appears in various descriptions of loneliness, which tend to have a clearly negative or a clearly positive trait. Indeed, it might seem odd that a single phenomenon can give rise to such conflicting portrayals. In Lord Byron's *Childe Harold's Pilgrimage*, solitude is the state 'when we are least alone'.[18] John Milton writes in *Paradise Lost* that 'solitude sometimes is best society'.[19] On the other hand, the definition of 'alone' in Ambrose Bierce's *Devil's Dictionary* is: 'In bad company'.[20] And Samuel Butler describes the melancholic as someone who has landed in the world's worst society: his own.[21] These authors are barely writing about the same thing, even though they use the same expressions.

The English language distinguishes between loneliness and solitude. It seems that earlier, these expressions were used more interchangeably; eventually, however, they crystallized in a clearer evaluative difference, where loneliness more often indicates a negative emotional state, and solitude a positive one. However, there are exceptions, such as in Duke Ellington's sorrowful jazz standard 'Solitude', in which the narrator is haunted by memories of a love who has left, and whose despair is so great that he fears he will go insane. In the psychological and sociological literature, loneliness receives far more attention than solitude, whereas the picture is less one-sided in philosophical writings.

One can be alienated without being aware of it, but hardly lonely, because by definition the emotion implies a discomfort or pain caused by some deficiency in one's relationship to others. Longing is a necessary component of loneliness. Longing implies a wish to overcome the physical or mental distance between yourself and someone you care about. It is the desire for someone's presence, for a departed family member or friend, for a child who has moved away, an absent parent, a girlfriend or boyfriend who has ended the relationship. It can also be a yearning for a greater closeness to someone who is actually present, such as in a marriage where the two parties have grown apart. Longing can also be unspecific, manifesting in the form of a desire to be close to someone, without having a clear idea of who that might be. Without such longing, which itself is painful, a person can be alone – but not lonely. Indeed, some people can be diagnosed as 'socially anhedonic'. Generally speaking, these people do not desire social contact, thereby distinguishing themselves from people with social anxiety, who have far more ambivalence in the social realm, where they both desire and fear social contact. A person with social anhedonia will experience little to no need for social contact, and consequently will not be disposed to experience loneliness.

As previously mentioned, loneliness is an emotional response to the fact that a person's need for connection to others is not satisfied. It is important to keep in mind that loneliness is an emotion, because it is often confused with other phenomena – with aloneness especially. However, being alone and being lonely are two distinct phenomena. They are both logically and empirically independent of each other. We can describe loneliness as a social withdrawal: a feeling of discomfort that informs us our need for relationships is not being met. We can also describe it as a social pain. Indeed, this feeling of social pain is related to physical pain; both seem to follow the same neurological pathways.[22] As with physical pain, social pain prompts a removal from the cause of the pain, namely, the social realm. We also find that there are a number of character traits that correlate strongly to loneliness, and that these character traits complicate our ability to form ties to others. As such, loneliness can have a self-reinforcing tendency.

The Philosophy of Loneliness

Loneliness is the subject of so much reflection because we all know it at first hand. Nonetheless, these first-hand experiences are not so reliable when it comes, for example, to understanding what causes loneliness. Not only can a person not make inferences from his or her own experiences to those of other people, but we also fail to grasp our own experiences adequately. If we want to say something of greater validity than simply to report our own experiences, more than mere introspection is required. At this point we must turn to the extensive body of research available in the field, with an abundance of empirical data from sociology, psychology and neuroscience.[23] An adequate philosophical exploration of loneliness must also take into account the empirical findings made by other disciplines in recent years – and which on several key points correct earlier perceptions of loneliness. As a result, this book will be characterized as much by various empirical findings as it is by the kind of conceptual analysis that many associate with philosophical works.

As such, one might ask why this book is entitled *A Philosophy of Loneliness*. What makes it a philosophical book? Perhaps the most obvious answer is that this book is written by a philosopher and it draws heavily on works written by other philosophers. Nonetheless, the distinction between what is philosophy and what is not philosophy is not entirely obvious. It is striking how in the last ten to fifteen years a number of philosophical disciplines have incorporated insights from the empirical sciences, especially considering that twentiethcentury philosophy by and large tried to limit itself to logic and conceptual analysis. If we look at the history of philosophy, however, we find that it is the rule rather than the exception for philosophy to incorporate the empirical sciences – indeed, the distinction between philosophy and science is also rather recent – and this new turn towards empirical sciences can be regarded as a return to a traditional mode of philosophy, rather than a radical departure from philosophy as such.

The book itself is organized into eight chapters. Chapter One provides an account of loneliness that is based more on sources from psychology and social science than from philosophy, but it also clarifies a number of concepts – such as the difference between being alone and being lonely – and gives an overview of different types of loneliness. It is, we find, an affective component that ultimately separates aloneness from loneliness, and in order to understand this idea better, Chapter Two provides a short discussion on the nature of emotions, and places emphasis on loneliness as an emotion. In Chapter Three I take a closer look at who is lonely, as well as the kinds of factor that particularly seem to promote the experience of loneliness. In this context, a lack of trust appears to be perhaps the most important factor in explaining both individual loneliness and the difference in loneliness's prevalence throughout various countries. Therefore, trust is the theme of Chapter Four. Is loneliness, furthermore, the opposite of love and friendship? In order to understand loneliness better, I will say more in Chapter Five about the role friendship and love play in human life. Loneliness, for its part, can shed light on why these phenomena are so vital to a meaningful life and to our happiness. In much of the literature on loneliness, however, modern individualism is highlighted as one of the main causes of loneliness. As such, we take a closer look at the modern individual in Chapter Six, considering what manner of creature we are dealing with and whether s/he is particularly haunted by loneliness. Chapter Seven follows with a presentation and discussion of solitude as a positive form of loneliness. Indeed, perhaps the main problem we are facing today is not that loneliness is on the rise, but rather that solitude is too scarce. Finally, there is a concluding discussion about the individual responsibility each one of us has for managing our loneliness.

ONE

The Essence of Loneliness

The whole conviction of my life now rests upon the belief
that loneliness, far from being a rare and curious phenomenon, peculiar to myself and to a few other solitary men, is
the central and inevitable fact of human existence. When
we examine the moments, acts, and statements of all kinds
of people – not only the grief and ecstasy of the greatest
poets, but also of the huge unhappiness of the average soul,
as evidenced by the innumerable strident words of abuse,
hatred and contempt, mistrust, and scorn that forever grate
upon our ears as the manswarm passes us in the streets
– we find, I think, that they are all suffering from the same
thing. The final cause of their complaint is loneliness.

THOMAS WOLFE, *The Hills Beyond*

There are various definitions of loneliness, but they do have
some things in common: a sense of pain or sadness, a perception of oneself as being isolated or alone, and a perceived
lack of closeness to others. Most definitions are variants of
these basic traits. Such definitions, however, leave the door
open as to whether the emotion has internal or external causes
– whether it is the result of the individual's own constitution
or the conditions under which he or she lives. In contrast, it
does not work to define loneliness, as does the Norwegian
Institute of Public Health, in terms of failed social support
or the like, for the simple reason that there are also people
with adequate social support, as we typically understand it,

who nonetheless suffer from chronic loneliness.[1] On the other hand, there are numerous people who experience poor social support but who are not plagued by loneliness. Statistical relationships between social support and loneliness do exist, but there is not a necessary connection, and loneliness must therefore be defined based on subjective experience rather than objective determinants such as a lack of social support.

'Lonely' and 'Alone'

The first recorded use of the word 'lonely' in English occurs in Shakespeare's *Coriolanus* and is used to indicate the state of utter aloneness. This fact might lead us to assume that loneliness is largely synonymous with aloneness, and indeed the idea does seem to be widespread that people who are lonely are more alone, and that those who are alone more often are lonelier. However, as we shall see, loneliness is logically and empirically independent from aloneness. What matters is not the extent to which an individual is surrounded by other people – or animals, as the case may be – but rather how that individual experiences his relationship to others.

We can say that every person is alone when it comes to experiencing the world. When you listen to a lecture, surrounded by hundreds of other people, you are in a certain sense alone with the words you are hearing. At a large concert, though surrounded by thousands, you are alone with the music, because it concerns *your* experience of it. Obviously, we also share these experiences with others – we process their reactions and communicate ours with words, we mime and gesture our experience of the lecture or concert – but our experience will always contain a private component that cannot fully be shared with others. Pain, for its part, cannot be shared. When it becomes strong enough, pain destroys a person's world and language. Pain pulverizes speech.[2] One can *say* that something hurts, but when the pain becomes too great, even that ability is lost. Great pain cannot be shared with others, simply because there is no room for anything else when pain becomes one's entire world. Of course, we can do more than imagine others' pain – we can also feel it to some extent, because it hurts when we realize that another person is suffering. Nonetheless, there is a chasm between the pain another person feels and our reaction to that pain. Such experiences show the impenetrable gulf that exists between ourselves and everyone else.

We are all alone in a certain sense. This is the thought that strikes Celia in T. S. Eliot's *The Cocktail Party* (1949) after Edward, her lover, decides to return to his wife. She says that the break-up has not simply left her alone right at that moment, but rather has made her aware that she has always been alone, that she will always be alone, and that this realization does not merely concern her relationship to Edward but to every single person: people are always alone, they make sounds and engage in mimicry, and they believe they are communicating with and understanding each other, but in reality all that is just an illusion.[3] Even though Celia uses the word 'alone' here, it is loneliness she is describing, the painful feeling of being disconnected from others. And Celia is right that, in a certain sense, we are born, live and die alone. We all have a self that relates to itself and is conscious of its separation from others.

Indeed, one can experience a metaphysical loneliness, where one believes oneself doomed to be perpetually lonely, cut off from others because the world is structured so that we are all ultimately left to our own devices.[4] A related variant is epistemic loneliness, which is the conviction that one can never communicate with or understand any other person, and that therefore one certainly cannot be understood by others. Bertrand Russell writes about such forms of loneliness in his autobiography:

> Everyone who realizes at all what human life is must
> feel at some time the strange loneliness of every sep-
> arate soul; and then the discovery in others of the
> same loneliness makes a new strange tie, and a growth
> of pity so warm as to be almost a compensation for
> what is lost.[5]

Paradoxically enough, the insight that every person is a lonely creature reveals for Russell a connection between people that is almost capable of overcoming loneliness. Such experiences and thoughts concern something far different than mere aloneness.

'Alone' is basically a numerical and physical term that indicates nothing beyond the fact that a person is not surrounded by others, and the word makes no evaluation about whether that fact is positive or negative. In context, 'alone' can certainly attain value, such as when one declares 'I am entirely alone' in a tone that reveals one's emotional state as either dejected or upbeat. 'Lonely', on the other hand, is always value-laden. For the most part, 'lonely' is used to express a negative state. On the other hand, one can also talk about 'enjoying being alone'. That is to say, 'lonely' contains an emotional dimension that 'alone' does not necessarily possess.

We can distinguish between different forms of aloneness depending on the type of relationship one has to others in that state. We can choose to be alone by heading off into nature, for example, away from others. There is also an institutional-ized form of aloneness, which recognizes a person's right to a private life. Private life, after all, is an institution whereby the social community remains intact, even though a person is permitted to withdraw from it. Finally, a person can be alone because he is socially isolated, where the desire for social relationships remains unfulfilled.

There are people who, typically speaking, spend all their time alone without being plagued by loneliness, and others who feel exceptionally lonely though they are surrounded by friends and family most of the time. Indeed, an average person spends almost 80 per cent of their waking hours together with others.[6] That is also true of the lonely. If we consider the group of people who on different surveys answer that they feel lonely 'often' or 'very often', it is a common feature that these people spend no more time alone than the group who answer that they do not feel lonely.[7] Indeed, in a review of over four hundred essays devoted to the experience of loneliness, one researcher found no correlation at all between the degree of physical isolation and the intensity of the loneliness felt.[8] As such, the actual number of people by whom a person is surrounded is uncorrelated to the emotion of loneliness. There are certain indications, however, that the strongest experiences of loneliness occur in situations where the lonely individual is, in fact, surrounded by others. Being alone and being lonely are logically and empirically independent from each other.

In news reports dwelling on loneliness, usually around holidays such as Christmas and Easter, the people featured are often those who are both alone and lonely. This helps create the impression that those people are lonely because they are alone. Indeed, that can seem logical. Certainly when it comes to elderly individuals who have lost a spouse, it seems clear that their loneliness is largely due to aloneness. Nonetheless, it would be premature to conclude that people who are alone and lonely are lonely because they are alone. The opposite can also be the case. As we will see, lonely individuals have character traits that complicate their ability to form connections with other people. Loneliness as such cannot be predicted by the number of people that surround an individual, but by whether the social interactions that individual has satisfy his or her desire for connection; that is, by whether they interpret those social interactions as meaningful.[9] Loneliness is a subjective phenomenon. It is experienced as a lack of satisfying relationships to others, whether because the subject has too few relationships or because their existing relationships do not provide the desired form of closeness.

In order to explain the contingent relationship between social isolation and loneliness, the so-called cognitive discrepancy model of loneliness was developed.[10] According to this theory, individuals develop an inner standard or expectation against which they measure their relationships to others. If their relationships meet this standard, they will be satisfied with those relationships and will not experience loneliness. Conversely, they will experience loneliness if those relationships do not meet that standard. In the meantime, multiple studies have, surprisingly, discovered that loneliness actually increases when a person has *more* friends than what he or she considers ideal.[11]

The four people closest to an individual in their social network provide the strongest protection against loneliness, and additional relationships yield only marginally better protection.[12] One will also be less likely to feel lonely if one has diverse relationships, with stronger ties to some and looser ties to others, and is connected to both friends and family. When asked which they prefer, most people unambiguously respond that they prefer a smaller number of closer friends instead of a larger number who are less close.[13] The quality of social networks is more important than their quantity, but under otherwise identical conditions, people with larger social networks are less lonely than people with smaller ones.

One social cognitive theory of loneliness considers loneliness to be generated by higher sensitivity to social threats.[14] That is to say, lonely people fear a lack of connection to others, and therefore look for signs of failure in their relationships, which in turn undermines their connections to others, additionally reinforcing loneliness. Social rejection, furthermore, creates sensitivity to new rejections, and may again prompt a person to look for new signs of rejection. That creates a norm of caution over spontaneity in social situations, which leads to a behaviour that can increase the risk of new rejections. In Chapter Three we will examine empirical evidence that supports such a social cognitive theory.

Loneliness and Life Meaning

It is an established fact that both chronic loneliness and experimentally induced social isolation are connected to lower levels of experienced life meaning.[15] Life meaning can of course be studied from a variety of different approaches, but a common attribute seems to be that a person's relationships to others plays a decisive role.[16] Without these relationships, existence seems to collapse. As William James so precisely observes:

> No more fiendish punishment could be devised, were such a thing physically possible, than that one should be turned loose in society and remain absolutely unnoticed by all the members thereof. If no one turned round when we entered, answered when we spoke, or minded what we did, but if every person we met 'cut us dead,' and acted as if we were nonexisting things, a kind of rage and impotent despair would ere long well up in us, from which the cruellest bodily tortures would be a relief; for these would make us feel that, however bad might be our plight, we had not sunk to such a depth as to be unworthy of attention at all.[17]

It would be intolerable to live in a world where one's existence, where one's being or non-being, seemed completely irrelevant to everyone else. As Dostoevsky's underground man writes: 'At that time I was only twenty-four. My life was even then gloomy, ill-regulated, and as solitary as that of a savage. I made friends with no one and positively buried myself more and more in my hole.'[18] He feels that his colleagues view him with disgust, and he regards them with both fear and contempt. Even as he cultivates such distance, however, he is also desperate for attention, and he tries to start fights simply so someone will take notice of him.

As Kierkegaard formulates it, the self is a relation that relates to itself,[19] but it also relates to other selves that relate to their own selves in turn. We are capable of considering what others think and feel about us, and we find other people's evaluations of us meaningful. Not meriting other people's attention is, therefore, destructive to our self-relation. People are essentially social beings, a fact which is indisputable. In studies of subjective well-being, a life partner and friends have far greater impact than do wealth or fame. As we shall see, social isolation therefore has an extremely negative effect on both psychic and somatic health. Banishment from society has long been regarded as one of the harshest punishments a person can suffer, and in antiquity it was considered almost as severe as the death penalty. In today's prisons, isolation is seen by many as a gruesome form of punishment.

Adam Smith writes about how 'the horror of solitude' forces us to seek out other people, even when, for example, we are ashamed and want to escape the judgemental gaze of others.[20] He emphasizes that those who grow up in solitude will never learn to know themselves.[21] And those who live in solitude will misjudge themselves, and overvalue both the good deeds they have done and the damage they have suffered.[22] We need the eyes of others upon us. British Enlightenment philosophy consistently emphasizes the dark and destructive side of loneliness. Anthony Ashley Cooper, 3rd Earl Shaftesbury, writes that humans are more incapable than any other creature of tolerating loneliness.[23] Edmund Burke describes total solitude as the greatest imaginable pain, because an entire life spent in such a state conflicts with our life's very purpose.[24] John Locke is clear in his evaluation of loneliness as an unnatural human state. God so created man in such a way that he is forced into fellowship with others of his own kind.[25] Loneliness, on the other hand, can be described as a dangerous state where emotions can easily take control of one's mind.[26] Similarly, David Hume writes:

> A perfect solitude is, perhaps, the greatest punishment we can suffer. Every pleasure languishes when enjoyed apart from company, and every pain becomes more cruel and intolerable. Whatever other passions we may be actuated by; pride, ambition, avarice, curiosity, revenge or lust; the soul or animating principle of them all is sympathy; nor would they have any force, were we to abstract entirely from the thoughts and sentiments of others. Let all the powers and elements of nature conspire to serve and obey one man: Let the sun rise and set at his command: The sea and rivers roll as he pleases, and the earth furnish spontaneously whatever may be useful or agreeable to him: He will still be miserable, till you give him some one person at least, with whom he may share his happiness, and whose esteem and friendship he may enjoy.[27]

As such, Hume regards the kind of solitude praised by religious thinkers as completely unnatural, much like celibacy, fasting and other things.[28]

There are evolutionary explanations for loneliness that emphasize the fact that we have developed to live in groups, together with others.[29] Undoubtedly, there are good evolutionary reasons to live in groups, such as the fact that one enjoys better protection from predators and can share resources. However, compelling evolutionary reasons can also be found for a creature not to live in a group, such as the fact that it makes hiding from predators easier, there is no sharing of resources, and there is no need to struggle for a place in the group hierarchy.[30] We also find that some species are more closely tied to groups than others. For example, we observe that chimpanzees are group animals to a greater extent than are orang-utans. Through a biological lens we can always say that it is 'natural' for humans to seek a social community, but it does not therefore follow that it is 'unnatural' to desire solitude or that spending a lot of time alone is necessarily negative for a person. It depends on how the individual relates to that condition.

For most of us our connection to a limited number of people constitutes the majority of our life meaning. Indeed, much of the meaning in our existence seems to disappear when we lose one of our nearest and dearest. Just how much of our life meaning is bound up with our relationship to them is, unfortunately, often clear only after we have lost them. As John Bowlby writes:

> Intimate attachments to other human beings are the hub around which a person's life revolves, not only when he is an infant or a toddler or a school-child but throughout his adolescence and his years of maturity as well, and on into old age. From these intimate attachments a person draws his strength and enjoyment of life . . .[31]

Bowlby is perhaps a degree more unequivocal than he ought to be, because some people's lives revolve around something other than attachments to others – for example, a researcher who spends almost all his or her time and attention on a research subject or a musician who is far more connected to his or her instrument than to any other person – but for most of us, Bowlby's description is quite accurate. That is why it is so painful when we fail to create and maintain those attachments.

The Forms of Loneliness

We can distinguish between chronic, situational and transient loneliness.[32] As the name suggests, chronic loneliness is a condition in which the subject experiences constant pain on account of having insufficient ties to others. Situational loneliness is caused by life changes, such as when a close friend or a family member dies, a romantic relationship ends, children move away from home and so on. A glimpse into this type of loneliness can be found, for example, in Roland Barthes' *Mourning Diary*, which he wrote following the death of his mother, with whom he had lived his entire life. Barthes confesses,

> A cold winter night. I'm warm enough, yet I'm alone. And I realize that I'll have to get used to existing quite naturally within this solitude, functioning there, working there, accompanied by, fastened to the 'presence of absence'.[33]

Transient loneliness can overtake us at any moment, whether we are at a crowded party or home alone. Situational loneliness, for its part, can be more intense than chronic loneliness, since it is due to a life upheaval and constitutes an experience of loss. However, because it can be attributed to a specific event – for example, a divorce or a death – we can also imagine that situational loneliness, in contrast to chronic loneliness, may be overcome by forming attachments to new people. On the other hand, the loss experience can be so powerful that it actually becomes impossible to form new ties. A literary example of this is Haruki Murakami's protagonist Tsukuru Tazaki, whose four closest – and only – friends suddenly inform him that they have no desire to see him or talk to him again.[34] This experience shapes the rest of the man's life and all of his relationships – both to himself and others – and he is never really able to form attachments again.

Situational loneliness, we find, is due to external causes. Chronic loneliness, in contrast, seems to be rooted in the self, because external changes in circumstance make so little impact on it. Therefore, we can perhaps distinguish between endogenous and exogenous loneliness, depending on whether the loneliness emotion has its main cause in the subject or in his or her surroundings. Of course, it will often be difficult to determine to what extent the loneliness emotion is endogenous or exogenous, simply because it is a relational phenomenon whose subject experiences an unfulfilled need for attachment to others. Nonetheless, the distinction does have a certain plausibility. A person who is plagued by loneliness throughout his or her life, no matter what their surroundings and even with a loving family and a solid social network, should presumably be placed in the endogenous category. On the other hand, a person who previously has not had problems with loneliness but who has been struck by the feeling after being a victim of social exclusion, perhaps of bullying, should be placed in the exogenous category. In most cases, however, it would be logical to include both internal and external causes. Indeed, any attempt to determine to what extent internal or external, characterological or situational variables have the strongest predictive force will show that both parts are needed to explain loneliness.[35]

The sociologist Robert S. Weiss distinguishes between social and emotional loneliness.[36] Social loneliness is a lack of social integration, and the socially lonely desire to be part of a community. In contrast, the emotionally lonely lack a close relationship to someone specific. According to Weiss, these two forms are distinct – they are qualitatively different. A person can suffer from one form of loneliness without suffering from the other, and can relieve one form without relieving the other. He or she can find a place in a community, and still feel emotionally lonely. On the other hand, a person can develop a close attachment to someone and still suffer

29

from social loneliness.[37] If an individual's partner or spouse is away for a time, emotional loneliness can make itself felt – they miss the close relationship in their existence, and contact via telephone or email is no adequate substitute. Furthermore, trips to the cinema or to concerts with friends can fulfil much of one's social requirements and also provide distraction from the loved one's absence, but friends are no substitute for the significant other. As the saying goes: 'Absence makes the heart grow fonder.' Separation increases the joy we take in those we care about. On the other hand, as Charlie Brown puts it: 'Absence makes the heart grow fonder, but it sure makes the rest of you lonely.'

We can take the other into our loneliness and relate to them mentally in a manner that is unobtainable when they are actually present. Loneliness creates a space in which we can reflect on our relationship to others, and feel how much we actually need them. In modern marriage and cohabitation, we find a development where the relationship to the partner displaces other social relationships, allowing social loneliness to arise even though the need for emotional closeness is satisfied. Similarly, children need both same-age friends and caring parental figures. A child who lacks one of these will suffer from substantial deprivation. If a child is socially isolated at school, a caring parent can improve the situation, but the parent is no adequate replacement for same-aged friends. In contrast, good school chums are no substitute for an emotionally absent parent.[38] Furthermore, there seems to be a difference in age when it comes to which form of loneliness will dominate: among younger people, it is social loneliness, and among older, emotional.[39] Nevertheless it ought to be underscored that emotional and social loneliness typically occur together.

Loneliness and Health

In the mass media, loneliness is often represented as a public disease or a public health problem. However, loneliness is not a disease, but a general human phenomenon. To experience the social hunger that loneliness implies is no more a sickness than feeling physically hungry because you have not eaten. However, loneliness can also develop such that it dramatically increases the risk of both mental and somatic disorders. Lonely individuals consume health services at a higher rate than do non-lonely individuals.[40] A meta-study of 148 studies examining the relationship between loneliness and health showed that loneliness was a strong mortality predictor, even though, for methodological reasons, suicide-related deaths were not considered.[41] The effect on mortality risk can be compared to smoking ten to fifteen cigarettes a day, and is greater than the impact of obesity or physical inactivity. Loneliness affects blood pressure and the immune system, and causes an increase of stress hormones in the body.[42] It also increases the risk of dementia, and generally weakens the cognitive faculties over time. Loneliness also appears to speed up the ageing process.[43] Lonely people sleep just as much as do non-lonely people, but they experience lower sleep quality and wake more often.[44] It is the subjective emotion of loneliness, as mentioned earlier, not the actual quantity of social support, that is correlated to poorer mental and somatic health.[45] As such, if we are to predict negative health outcomes, then subjective social isolation – that is, a person's feeling of loneliness – is a much more precise variable than objective social isolation, that is, a person who is alone.

Loneliness is not a psychiatric diagnosis, nor should it become one. Loneliness can become pathological, when the chronic and painful experience of being unable to truly form ties with someone affects a person's every relationship, so that the lonely person will interpret every relationship to others as lacking in closeness. Nonetheless, loneliness as such is not a pathological phenomenon, just as not all shyness can be regarded as social anxiety. I will not discuss loneliness in the context of psychiatric diagnoses such as social anxiety or the Jungian distinction between introvert and extrovert personalities.[46] I will, however, briefly remark that a high degree of loneliness is strongly correlated to meeting the criteria for depression, but even then it is basically unclear which is the cause and which is the effect – or whether there is even a causal relationship, for that matter. Nevertheless, it has been demonstrated that loneliness can be used to predict an increase in depressive symptoms, but depressive symptoms are no predictor of loneliness.[47] Ultimately, these are two distinct conditions, and a person can be lonely without being depressed and depressed without being lonely. Furthermore, strong correlations exist between loneliness and suicidal thoughts and behaviours.[48]

Loneliness appears to have consequences for our capacity to function in daily life. The psychologists Roy Baumeister and Jean Twenge have conducted multiple experiments exploring the effects contained in the experience of social exclusion.[49] In one experiment, students were assembled in small groups and were given fifteen minutes to get acquainted with each other. After that they were separated and asked to write down the names of two people from that group with whom they wished to work. Finally, they were randomly sorted into two groups again, with one group being told that everyone wanted to work with them, and the others told that no one wanted to work with them. In another experiment, students were given personality tests, and afterwards one group was informed that they would have good relationships, friends and family in their lives, while the other group was told they were doomed to loneliness. A third group, which was the control group, was told that their lives would be full of upheaval. Baumeister and Twenge have also conducted a number of other, similar experiments. The central question is what effect hearing that they had been or would be socially excluded had on these students. The results were that: 1) they became more aggressive, not merely towards the people who had hurt them, but also towards others; 2) they made self-destructive decisions; 3) they performed poorly on tests of rational ability; 4) they gave up demanding tasks more quickly. Baumeister and Twenge concluded that social exclusion cripples our capacity to self-regulate. Obviously, self-regulation is a central component of our relationships to others, and it appears that any weakening in our relationships to others – even the perception of such a weakening – cripples our ability or our will to regulate ourselves. There is also evidence that people who feel lonely in their job perform worse at work than people who do not feel lonely.[50]

Loneliness itself should not be regarded as a disease. After all, everyone experiences it occasionally and it can be regarded as a natural component of our emotional defence system. Furthermore, just as fear is not a disease, loneliness is not itself pathological. However, just as the emotion of fear can develop along pathological lines, becoming too strong and excessive, such that a person's functionality is severely weakened, loneliness can also develop in a similar way. In this case, loneliness implies enormous consequences for a person's mental and somatic health.

TWO

Loneliness as Emotion

Who knows what true loneliness is – not the conventional word, but the naked terror? To the lonely themselves it wears a mask. The most miserable outcast hugs some memory or some illusion. Now and then a fatal conjunction of events may lift the veil for an instant. For an instant only. No human being could bear a steady view of moral solitude without going mad.

JOSEPH CONRAD, *Under Western Eyes*

Loneliness has both an affective and a cognitive side. These two sides are not sharply divided, however, since affective phenomena have cognitive aspects and vice versa. What you feel depends on how you process your experience, and how you process your experience depends on what you feel. Within the realm of loneliness studies, it varies significantly as to whether it is the affective or the cognitive aspect that receives the most emphasis – whether the felt lack of an adequate connection to others is given weight or whether the perceived incongruity between the desired connection and the actual connection is stressed. Nevertheless, an adequate understanding of the phenomenon requires both dimensions to be incorporated. However, it is the affective component, the actual emotion of loneliness, that is correlated to increased incidences of somatic and psychological disorders, and this is the component that makes loneliness what it is – something more than simply being alone.

What are Emotions?

Most books dealing with the philosophy or psychology of emotion do not have a chapter on loneliness. And most of the time the subject is completely excluded or mentioned only in passing. Fear occupies a prominent place in such works, as do anger and love, but not loneliness. Why is that? The phenomenon, after all, is not marginal. Could it perhaps be that loneliness is essentially regarded not as an emotion, but rather as a social problem? For my part, I consider loneliness to be an emotional response to the fact that one's desire for a connection to others is not satisfied. That which makes loneliness loneliness – as something other than being alone or having poor social support – is the phenomenon's affective or emotional dimension.

In his excellent book *The Subtlety of Emotions*, Aaron Ben-Ze'ev points out that everyday language does not clearly distinguish between what qualifies as an emotion and what does not. For example, it is unclear to what extent surprise, loneliness and aesthetic experiences qualify as emotions, while it is commonly accepted that fear, anger and jealousy do qualify.[1] Ben-Ze'ev himself regards loneliness as an emotion, or more particularly, as a certain type of sadness 'which stems from the absence of desired social relationships'.[2] At the same time, it must be admitted that loneliness is not an emotion that receives especially broad or informative treatment in his work.

The terms 'feeling' and 'emotion' cover an extremely diverse set of phenomena ranging from pain, hunger and thirst to jealousy, envy and love, from the almost purely physiological to the almost completely cognitive. We tend to regard the former as being more 'physical' in character, while the latter we consider to be more 'cognitive'. The English language also differentiates between feelings and emotions, feelings being associated with more physical sensations and emotions with the more mental ones. There is significant disagreement about where exactly to draw the line between feelings and emotions, and which states belong to one category or the other. I have chosen not to make such a distinction, and primarily to use the term 'emotion'. Loneliness basically belongs more to the cognitive than to the physical end of the emotion continuum, but we also find that loneliness, as a social pain, appears to follow the same neural pathways as does physical pain.[3] Indeed, there is a startling connection between social and physical pain.[4] Studies have also explored whether medicine that is normally meant for physical pain can also be used to reduce social pain, and the answer is that it actually can.[5] (Of course, that does not mean that an aspirin a day will cure the problem of loneliness.)

The category of emotions is certainly not homogeneous and covers a wide array of phenomena. In my opinion, it is doubtful that any well-functioning definition could be found that provides the necessary and adequate conditions for when x is an emotion, but there is no shortage of interesting theories that attempt to do just that.[6] In emotion theories, it is common to emphasize the following characteristic: emotions are subjective phenomena. Typically, they have some valence, that is, they are either positive or negative, not neutral. An emotion has an intentional object, that is, it is about something or someone. Often, emotions are of rather short duration, and that duration will be determined by a shift in valence. Loneliness possesses all of these characteristics, except that it can be of extremely long duration and can occur in chronic forms. On the other hand, there are also chronic pains: one can experience hunger and thirst for long periods of time; and jealousy, envy and love can endure for years. For that reason, it is doubtful that short duration ought to be regarded as a central criterion for defining emotion – it can be characteristic of some emotions, and not of others.

It is also a matter of debate whether or not there is a set of basic emotions, that is, emotions that are not learned but that are innate, and that are common to people of all cultures.[7] In and of itself, the thought is not unreasonable, but there is disagreement concerning the number of basic emotions that exist and what exactly they are. Anger, fear, happiness, disgust and surprise are typically mentioned, but it is striking just how wide the disagreement is concerning which emotions belong on such a list. For example, a survey of fourteen lists containing 'basic emotions' shows that there is not a single emotion common to every list.[8] Furthermore, it is difficult to adequately distinguish between the biological, psychological and social aspects of emotions. Every emotion undoubtedly has a biological basis, but emotions are also shaped by individual experiences and social norms. Every emotion also has an evolution, a social and a personal history, and if we are to understand that emotion we must account for all three aspects. Emotions appear to us as 'natural' and spontaneous, but they are also individually and socially constructed.[9]

Some emotions are present from birth, while others develop over time. As such, it is not easy to determine when exactly a person is capable of experiencing loneliness. Relatively small children of preschool age are linguistically capable of expressing loneliness, but what about even younger children who have not yet developed the necessary language skills: can they feel loneliness? The answer is anything but simple. We believe we can identify complex emotions such as shame and envy in small children by their facial expressions, but there is no facial expression that corresponds to loneliness. What about a tiny child who cries when left alone? It is certainly conceivable that that child experiences loneliness, but it could also be a case of fear. Nonetheless, we can determine that the emotion of loneliness appears in early childhood.[10] After that it will more or less accompany a person for the rest of their life.

Emotional Interpretation

As Charles Taylor underscores, interpretation is constitutive for emotions.[11] There is no such thing as a 'raw' emotion. Yet it is not always obvious what a person's emotional state actually is. Two people can seem to experience the same emotion, but will use different terms to describe it. A person might be sad, and that sadness can be caused by a lack of connection to someone or by the sense that a connection to someone has been weakened, without that person therefore describing themselves as 'lonely'. A person might desire a friend, a love interest or a greater social community, and can express that emotion as longing rather than as loneliness. If a person's loved one dies, that person – even after a long period of time – will typically describe their emotion as sorrow rather than as loneliness, even though all the criteria for loneliness are met. The distinction between various emotional states can be extremely unclear. We might of course wish that the boundaries between emotions were clearer, and that we could perhaps develop a definition that gives the necessary and sufficient conditions, such that: 'x is lonely if, and only if . . .'. In reality, not all phenomena allow themselves to be defined in that way, and when we take up emotions in general, and loneliness in particular, we must accept a certain vagueness surrounding our object. As Aristotle puts it, it is 'a mark of an educated person to look in each area for only that degree of accuracy that the nature of the subject permits'.[12]

Indeed, we are not always entirely certain what our own emotional state is. Some emotions are considered shameful, and we are reluctant to admit to others that we feel them. Often, we will not even admit it to ourselves. It is well-established that loneliness is often considered shameful; this is something to which we shall return in Chapter Eight. As an emotion, loneliness tells us that our social life is not satisfying, and that painful sensation only increases when the fact becomes socially evident. Loneliness is something we hide. We can also hide it from ourselves.

Another similar example is envy, which causes those who feel it to appear to be contemptible. As François de La Rochefoucauld points out: 'We often pride ourselves on our passions, even the most criminal ones; but envy is a timid, shamefaced passion, which we never dare to acknowledge.'[13] Envy is such an unflattering emotion for our self-image that an individual will often interpret the emotion in another way, such as believing that the emotion's object deserves his resentment. Indeed, our capacity for self-deception is so well-developed that a person's perception of their own emotional states is anything but infallible.

It also happens that, in retrospect, we can reinterpret earlier emotional states. Returning home from a party, a person can find that, whereas at the party they thought everything was great, in reality they were bored to tears the whole evening. One can look back at a period in one's life and realize: 'At the time I thought I was happy, but I was actually extremely unhappy.' Similarly, one might reflect on an earlier phase of one's life and think: 'I was quite lonely at that time, even though I didn't realize it.' That idea would seem to create difficulties for an approach to loneliness that places such great emphasis upon the phenomenon as an emotion, because one certainly cannot have an emotion without feeling it: unfelt emotions do not exist. And that is certainly true, as far as it goes. However, one can push a feeling aside, so that it no longer occupies a central place in one's awareness, or one can interpret and conceptualize it as something else. It is not certain that a person will correctly identify an emotion when he or she is having it, but in order to be able to assert that person x has emotion y at point t, x must, at least in retrospect, be able to recognize y as an emotion he or she felt at t.

In order to be lonely, you have to feel lonely. To be lonely is to have a definite emotion. That emotion is a kind of sadness. I can *think* I am lonely without actually being in that state, but I cannot *feel* lonely without actually being lonely. The extent to which x is lonely is completely determined by the affective state in which x exists, and that is essentially independent of all objective determinants, such as whether x is socially isolated or not, whether x has close confidants, friends, family and so on.

The Function of Emotions

Let us now try and take a closer look at the function of an emotion such as loneliness. In this context, the term 'mood' can be useful. The distinction between emotions and moods is not so easy to draw, since they are related affective phenomena. A mood is more general, and it touches on the world as a whole. Emotions, in contrast, usually have one or more specific, intentional object(s). Often, a mood will endure longer than an emotion. There is a specific loneliness, such as when you have lost someone close to you, but there is also a vague loneliness where you are uncertain as to what or whom you are actually missing. The distinction between emotions and moods, however, is not especially critical to our subsequent discussion of loneliness as an affective phenomenon, and so I will discuss emotions and moods interchangeably.

Moods tell us *how* we are doing. And we always *are* some way or other. If someone asks you how you are doing, that question always has an answer, even if you do not necessarily give an honest one. Your answer can always be: 'I'm doing great.' To be 'doing great' is to be in an affective state, albeit not one of the most interesting ones imaginable. Emotions and moods are, according to Heidegger, not purely subjective; indeed, 'mood is precisely the basic way in which we are outside ourselves.'[14] At the same time, they give us contact with ourselves. An emotion grants you access to yourself and to the outside world, but precisely because the emotion contains the possibility of opening to such a degree, it can also be obscuring, and as such can provide an inadequate view of both yourself and the world.[15] Without moods, you would have no reason to orient yourself towards one thing instead of another, because a lack of mood would also be a lack of meaning. No experience exists without a mood, and if you tried to imagine such an experience, it would necessarily be incomprehensible, because it would lack all significance.

Moods disclose our relationship to the world, to other people and to ourselves, and different moods will reveal different worlds and different selves. Some moods, such as fear or boredom, reveal the world as distant, while others, such as happiness, reveal a closeness to the things of world. In the meantime, moods that unveil a closeness to things typically escape attention. In happiness your attention is focused on whatever gladdens you, while the alienation to things found in boredom makes it more likely that your attention is focused upon the mood itself. In loneliness your attention is typically directed towards the felt lack at its heart. Some moods open up sociability, while others lead to social withdrawal. Loneliness implies a longing for sociability, but in practice often leads to social withdrawal.

Loneliness as a World Perspective

Moods open up experiential space.[16] Heidegger mostly emphasizes the 'dark' moods, but he also discusses other moods, such as the extreme happiness produced by the presence of someone we love.[17] The mood of love opens the world to us as an object where love can occur. This happiness will reveal not simply something about the person we love, but about the world as a whole, because everything else will come to be experienced in the light of such joy. We have all experienced how different the world seems when we first fall in love and also when that love has passed. Heidegger protests against the saying that love makes us blind, and emphasizes instead that love prompts us to see things that we cannot see when we are not in love.[18] When you are in a bad mood, parts of the world are closed to you, and you are unable, for example, to delight in other people's joy. Therefore, it is fitting that the protagonist in Samuel Beckett's early novel *Dream of Fair to Middling Women* is described as suffering from a 'transcendental gloom', for that gloom is a condition of possibility for experiencing the world as he does.[19] In many philosophical texts, however, solitude is emphasized as a privileged space of reflection. Heidegger's writings are symptomatic of this position when he writes that solitude is the path to knowledge of the self.[20] Is it really the case that in solitude one approaches the truth more closely than otherwise? I do not believe so. Solitude might be able to afford you some insights which you otherwise would not have had, but it also obscures other insights. Solitude gives you *another* perspective on existence – not necessarily a truer one.

Moods do not merely accompany our being together with others, but in contrast go a long way towards determining *how* we are together with others.[21] This seems to be a key factor in loneliness's phenomenology. A person in a lonely mood will be together with others in a different way to someone who is not in that mood. We can say that the lonely and the non-lonely occupy different worlds, so to speak, because the difference in mood will result in them having very different experiences of the world, each other, and the situations in which they find themselves. In *Tractatus logico-philosophicus* (1921), Ludwig Wittgenstein writes: 'The world of the happy man is a different one from that of the unhappy man.'[22] The same could be said of the lonely person's world. Loneliness shows you a lonely part of reality. It shows you a lonely world. However, there are other parts – or other worlds, if you will.

Emotions can therefore be regarded not simply as purely subjective occurrences, but as cognitive instruments, that is, as tools that tell us something about reality. Like all other instruments we use to perceive reality, emotions can also provide us with a correct or an erroneous view. What we feel in a situation depends upon how we interpret that situation. As we shall see in Chapter Three, there are differences in how the lonely and the non-lonely interpret social situations. There is a clear correlation, for example, between low levels of trust and loneliness. Lonely individuals interpret their social surroundings as threatening to a greater extent than non-lonely individuals.[23] They also regard social situations as being risk-filled to a greater degree than do non-lonely individuals, and that causes them to enter social situations differently, which in turn proves an obstacle to forming the attachments they so desire. Fear prevents the very thing that could make their loneliness subside: human contact. Social fear, that is, undermines immediacy in our relationships to other people, and, from this perspective, undermines social relationships. When a lonely person enters a social situation with fear, that fear contains a projection about that particular future situation emerging as a source of pain or harm. As Aristotle writes: 'Fear may be defined as a pain or disturbance due to a mental picture of some destructive or painful evil in the future.'[24] It is evident that a person who enters a social situation with such an attitude will be more reserved than a person with a carefree attitude, and that will impose boundaries on the types of attachment that person can form. In this context, the idea of psychic equivalence becomes relevant. The concept affirms that a person does not have the capacity to distinguish between their inner emotional or cognitive states and an objective reality. In short, a person concludes from whatever he or she feels about something that the emotion *is* the reality. For example, a person can conclude from their own emotion of insecurity that other people are hostile, even if that is not actually the case.

One can hold that lonely people more often draw inadequate, emotional conclusions about social situations.

However, the lonely person can object that he or she is hardly out of touch with the situation, because every meeting with another person does imply the possibility of painful rejection. Still, the response might be that this very fear of rejection increases the chances of being rejected. As Aristotle writes: 'One kind of missing the mark is to fear the wrong thing, another to fear in the wrong way, another to fear at the wrong time, and so on.'[25] One can, for that matter, feel excessive fear in relation to an object that does contain a certain degree of risk, but where one's fear is not in logical proportion to the risk.

As I have pointed out, loneliness can be described as social withdrawal, a feeling of discomfort or pain that informs us that our need for attachment to others is not satisfied. In this context, dysfunctional traits can also make an appearance. One can imagine the emotion lasting, even though an individual *is* apparently attached to others to a large extent, as part of a social community or having close confidants. Eventually, one can imagine that the need becomes so great that it can never be satisfied. In fact, it has been documented that the chronically lonely have much higher expectations of interpersonal relationships than do not-lonely people.[26] They are social perfectionists who entertain higher demands, both for themselves and for others, in social interaction.[27] This idea will be discussed further in Chapter Three. For many chronically lonely people, however, the problem seems to be this: no matter what their social surroundings might be – whether or not they are constantly surrounded by caring and thoughtful friends and family – they still feel lonely. They harbour an expectation of attachment so strong that it can never be realized. No subsequent change in their social surroundings will be able to solve their loneliness problem. The solution must be found in the work the lonely person undertakes with him- or herself.

Shaping Emotional Life

When you are in a given mood, the world seems to hold a definite field of possibilities.[28] Different moods facilitate different relationships to the world as a whole, to objects and to other people. Moods, however, cannot simply be changed by an act of will. As Heidegger express it, you cannot simply slip a mood off and on as you do a pair of gloves.[29] At the same time, he writes that we should try to control our moods, but does not offer many suggestions about how such control might be achieved.[30] Since we are essentially passive in relation to moods, it is anything but obvious how we are to obtain such control, but Heidegger seems to think that we should somehow be in a position to enter into a counter-mood.[31] In our context, the question then becomes: what is a counter-mood to loneliness? The sense of belonging? Such belonging is exactly what the lonely individual desires, but what he or she is unable to secure. We must proceed more indirectly, therefore, and, for example, learn to depend on others. As we shall see, a generalized mistrust of other people is one of the most important indicators of loneliness. If you learn to trust others, and to interpret their words, expressions and gestures as less threatening, you will also be able to relate more immediately to them, and therefore improve the conditions necessary for forming attachments.

Lonely persons have shaped a self that both fears other people and simultaneously desires attachment to them. At the same time, lonely persons could also have formed another self that would have related to its social surroundings in another way. However, it should be pointed out that none of us can simply choose an emotion. The lonely individual cannot simply choose not to feel fear or pain caused by lack of attachment. Meanwhile, we can influence our emotions in a more indirect fashion. You can always seek out a situation where a certain emotion arises, where you normally experience fear of rejection and the resulting loneliness. You can work with the emotions you bring to the situation and with the emotions that arise in that situation. You have a limited but nonetheless real ability to invite an emotion or to suppress it. We must all work with our emotional lives and must shape our emotional dispositions. For this reason, we can be said to bear a responsibility for our emotions. We all bear a responsibility whose subject and object is one and the same: *I* am responsible for *me*. I am responsible not only for what I do, but also in a certain sense for what I feel and believe, according to the thought that these emotions and beliefs can be either adequate or inadequate in relation to their objects, and furthermore, that it is in my power to modify them. Emotions are not simply given, but something with which each individual can work within themselves.

We evaluate emotional responses in a normative fashion, and we can find that someone feels too much or too little in a given situation. We can think that someone is not sad enough following a tragedy, that they are too angry about a trifling 'insult', or too jealous of a girlfriend or boyfriend who, judging by all the signs, is above suspicion. In the comedy series *Little Britain*, there is an older, dignified woman who is extremely racist, and if she, for example, has eaten a cake touched by a person of another skin colour, she feels so nauseous that she immediately throws up. We condemn a person who reacts that way, even though it is a spontaneous emotional reaction, because she *should not* feel that way, and we can blame her for not attempting to change the way she thinks and feels about people of another skin colour. Similarly, we can contend that a person's complaint of inadequate social support with an attendant emotion of loneliness is untenable, because that person has the social support it is reasonable to expect.

We cultivate feelings and develop emotional habits. By altering your evaluations, you can alter your emotions. You can change your practices and habits, and thereby also your emotions. All of our emotions are continually objects of regulation. What you feel is scarcely an object of choice there and then, but is a result of dispositions – both innate and acquired – and a series of choices that extend back over time. You are not responsible for the tendency to feel lonely, but you are responsible for how you manage that tendency. Therefore, you are, to some extent, responsible for your own loneliness. This is a theme to which we shall return in Chapter Eight.

THREE

Who are the Lonely?

Lonely people tend, rather, to be lonely because they decline
to bear the psychic costs of being around other humans.
They are allergic to people. People affect them too strongly.

DAVID FOSTER WALLACE, 'E Unibus Pluram:
Television and U.S. Fiction'

Who are the lonely and how many of them are there?
There is no straightforward way to answer this question.
Since loneliness, in contrast to being alone, is a subjective
phenomenon, it cannot be quantified on the basis of objective
criteria. Therefore, one must use subjective criteria, and the
number one ends up with clearly depends on which criteria
one puts in place. The most obvious approach is to ask people
if they feel or have ever felt lonely. And yet, when we distinguish between 'lonely' and 'non-lonely', it is anything but
obvious where the boundary should be drawn. In a certain
sense we are all lonely, but if we embrace such a broad conception of loneliness, we will not be able to separate out the most
severely affected. On the other hand, if we establish a strict
conception of loneliness, there will be very few people who
meet our criteria, and that could lead to us underestimating
the problem's extent.

Quantifying Loneliness

In an attempt to quantify loneliness, several tests have been developed. The most widespread is the UCLA Loneliness Scale, which has been employed since the end of the 1970s. However, a weakness associated with this particular test is that it seems to have been primarily developed with young, American students in mind, and it is questionable whether it is entirely applicable when it comes to other groups, such as Norwegian retirees or Chinese children. In addition, key terms employed by the test are substantially vague – respondents are asked to say whether they have 'sometimes' or 'often' felt completely alone. Yet where is the line to be drawn between 'sometimes' and 'often'? There is every reason to believe that one person's 'sometimes' is another person's 'often'. Therefore, more complex tests are desirable; two examples are the De Jong Gierveld Loneliness Scale and the Social and Emotional Loneliness Scale for Adults. Some tests are for more specific forms of loneliness, such as the Existential Loneliness Questionnaire. There is also a test for loneliness's positive form: the Preference for Solitude Scale.

Because we are dealing with a subjective phenomenon, however, it is doubtful that we will ever succeed in developing tools of measurement that employ high precision. Obviously, one can wish for more precise measurements, but if the actual phenomenon does not allow for it, there is nothing more to be done than to use the tools we have at hand while remaining conscious of their limits. As such, all results of surveys that explore the number of lonely individuals must be taken with a pinch of salt, simply because that number cannot be attained objectively. Furthermore, one must be wary of drawing conclusions regarding the extent to which the number has or has not risen, because small variations in the way in which questions are posed can substantially influence results.

Nonetheless, it is upon data from just such surveys that we must base our consideration. How does loneliness develop? Does it increase? The results are mixed. Some studies show a rise, others a reduction, and most little change. Most of these studies concentrate on the elderly, and these clearly demonstrate that elderly people are not more lonely than they were before.[1] There are also studies that show a significant increase in the loneliness count,[2] but these are exceptions, despite the fact they most often receive the greatest media attention. All told, the numbers seem to remain stable over time, but we should be wary of attempting to draw any foolproof conclusions.

Due to the low grade of precision among the measuring tools utilized, then, it is essentially meaningless to state that '*x* per cent of the population are lonely', because the accuracy of the statement is misleading. We can, however, use these surveys to inform ourselves about variations between different countries, social groups, age groups, genders and so on. We can also attempt to say something about the development of the prevalence of loneliness over time, but here we are also on uncertain ground, because we often have to rely on studies that are not equally structured and that subsequently yield figures that are difficult to compare.

Norwegian Loneliness

In Norway, thanks to comprehensive surveys on income and living conditions, we have a wealth of data from which to study loneliness and its correlations with other phenomena. The following is based on surveys of income and living conditions for the years 1980–2012.[3] All figures from the surveys are percentages; the surveys typically polled 6,000–8,000 people.

If we briefly summarize the findings of these surveys, we discover that loneliness has not increased among those surveyed. Almost the only change is a certain reduction in the percentage of respondents who claim to have experienced loneliness 'often' or that they are 'very much bothered' by it.

On the other hand, the figure that *has* significantly changed between 1980 and 2012 is the percentage of people who have a close confidant, as shown here:

	1980	1983	1987	1998	2002	2005	2008	2012
MEN	62	63	69	80	80	97	93	93
WOMEN	74	77	78	90	89	98	96	96

In the latest surveys, nearly all of those questioned responded that they had a confidant. When we investigate the correlation between the experience of loneliness and having a confidant, it is weak in the individual surveys. The increase in the number of people that have a confidant from the earlier to the latest surveys is, as we shall see, not accompanied by a corresponding reduction in the figures for experienced loneliness. Perhaps that means that having a confidant is less important in avoiding loneliness than has been typically assumed.

The extent to which an individual has contact with friends – either often or seldom – does not have a significant impact either. For those who respond that they 'often' feel lonely, it hardly makes a difference whether they meet with friends often or seldom. Meeting with friends, however, does have a certain impact among those who feel lonely 'now and then' or 'seldom'. This can support a hypothesis that 'chronic' loneliness is of the endogenous variety, and that it is not influenced so much by social surroundings, whereas these surroundings play a larger role for others. As a matter of interest, it can also be mentioned that those who meet with friends on a daily basis have a higher prevalence of loneliness than those who meet with friends less often.

There is little difference in the loneliness prevalence between small and large communities, but most surveys of income and living conditions yield a higher loneliness figure among respondents who live in areas with fewer inhabitants, while figures are a little lower in larger cities. In Norway, there is relatively little variation between different age groups compared to in other countries, but here we also find the highest rates in the age groups of 16–24 and 67-plus. In Norway, as in practically all other countries, there is a consistently higher loneliness prevalence among women than among men. This gender difference is so consistent that in what follows I have chosen to present separate figures for genders. A discussion of the possible reasons for this gender difference will be given later in the chapter.

The questions are also phrased rather differently in the oldest and newest surveys of income and living conditions. The oldest surveys enquire about the frequency with which loneliness is experienced and the newest about how plagued one is by it. These two things can be essentially independent, since it is conceivable that a portion of those who respond that they experience loneliness do not consider it troublesome, and, conversely, that people who experience loneliness more seldom find it extremely troubling. Meanwhile, we can conclude that there actually is a clear correlation between the results in the older and the newer surveys by examining figures from 1998, when both types of question were asked. However, we can also remark that only a little over half of those who responded that they experience loneliness 'often' said that they were 'very much bothered' by it. Therefore, I choose to present these figures in two different tables according to the type of question posed.

There is no strong developmental tendency in these figures as a whole. There appears to be a falling tendency in the proportion of those hardest hit, who answer that they experience loneliness 'often' or that they are 'very much bothered'. Otherwise, there is little change to note. We can, in any case, conclude that these surveys definitively do not support the claim that we are experiencing a loneliness epidemic. We

	Often	Sometimes	Seldom	Never
1991 – MEN	3.2	13.5	20.6	62.7
1991 – WOMEN	5.0	21.1	23.3	50.6
1995 – MEN	3.2	13.7	20.6	62.6
1995 – WOMEN	5.3	21.5	22.9	50.3
1998 – MEN	2.4	14.0	29.6	53.9
1998 – WOMEN	4.3	20.8	31.1	43.7

THE FEELING OF LONELINESS

	Extremely bothered	Very much bothered	Little bothered	Not bothered
1998 – MEN	1.5	3.5	17.2	77.8
1998 – WOMEN	2.4	4.2	22.1	71.4
2002 – MEN	1.5	2.9	16.2	79.4
2002 – WOMEN	2.2	3.6	20.8	73.3
2005 – MEN	1.2	2.5	15.8	80.5
2005 – WOMEN	1.6	4.0	19.2	75.3
2008 – MEN	1.2	3.0	18.0	77.8
2008 – WOMEN	1.3	4.1	23.8	70.8
2012 – MEN	1.0	3.4	17.7	77.9
2012 – WOMEN	1.8	5.5	23.3	69.5

can also conclude that the loneliness problem has a rather limited scope in the population.

When figures such as 'one in four Norwegians suffer from loneliness' appear, they are true, in and of themselves, because around that percentage of people do answer that they are 'extremely bothered', 'very much bothered' or 'little bothered' by loneliness. However, it is misleading to lump those three groups together. That is like lumping together a group of people with chronic migraines and a group who get a small headache every now and then, as if they were identical.

As already mentioned, I am therefore sceptical of claims that follow the pattern '*x* per cent of the population is lonely,' because the precision in the statement is deceptive when it comes to such a vague phenomenon as loneliness. After all, we all find ourselves at some place or other in that continuum.

Loneliness, Life Phases and Social Groups

In which life phase is it most typical to be bothered by loneliness? The answers given by different studies are scattered.[4] Most studies comparing different age groups show the highest levels among youths and the elderly; that is, there is a non-linear distribution, with the lowest levels being among those of working age. However, some studies also show the direct opposite, and some show hardly any difference among age groups.[5]

Loneliness among children is correlated with parental loneliness, and there is a stronger correlation with the mother's than with the father's.[6] Such correlation can have a variety of explanations, both of social and genetic character. Loneliness appears to be a partially inherited phenomenon, where genetics probably accounts for around half of the variation in the loneliness emotion; that is, it has a heritability of around 45–50 per cent.[7] One interesting trait is that the impact of inheritance seems to decrease dramatically between childhood and adolescence, and it is much weaker among twelve-year-olds than among seven-year-olds.

There are studies that suggest that a genetically determined deficiency in oxytocin receptors leads to a stronger feeling of loneliness.[8] Oxytocin is a key factor in the biochemical groundwork for the emotion of attachment to others. A deficiency in the ability to utilize oxytocin can therefore partially explain the loneliness emotion, although we also have to be wary of reducing so complex a phenomenon as loneliness to a receptoral deficiency.[9]

Some groups, furthermore, are overrepresented in these studies, such as immigrants, disabled people and the elderly. To be married or cohabiting, to have one or more close friends, good health and a high level of education seems typically to reduce the risk of loneliness. To exist completely outside the working world is correlated with higher loneliness, whereas unemployment is not as strongly correlated.[10] A peculiar gender difference is that men in the workplace have a lower level of loneliness, whereas women in the workplace have a higher level compared with men outside the working world.[11] Health does not make a large impact among the elderly, but otherwise poor health is correlated with loneliness.

When it comes to the extent to which an individual feels lonely, one of the key factors is that individual's country of residence. This actually has a greater influence than age. In Europe, Eastern European citizens are clearly the most lonely, whereas Northern Europeans are clearly the least lonely.[12] There is also a relatively high percentage in Southern European countries such as Italy, Greece and Portugal. The Scandinavian countries distinguish themselves with a relatively low prevalence compared to other European countries, and with relatively little variation in prevalence among different age groups.[13]

Loneliness and Gender

Women are the largest overrepresented group. Most studies show a higher prevalence of loneliness among women than men.[14] There is no difference in prevalence among genders in childhood, but thereafter there are significant differences at different ages and in all societies. There are some studies that show a higher prevalence of loneliness among men than women, but these are exceptions; a higher prevalence of loneliness among women, meanwhile, has been supported by meta-analyses, but the difference in prevalence is striking from one study to the next.[15] Some studies show that even though there is a higher prevalence among women than among men, the loneliness emotion is stronger in the men affected than among the women.[16] There also seems to be a gender difference in *when* loneliness increases after having abated during the working years. One study suggests that loneliness among men increases after the age of 75, and among women after the age of 55 – a dramatic difference.[17]

It is uncertain why more women than men respond that they experience loneliness, especially when it is well documented that women more often have a social network and close confidants. They also have greater contact with their families. Women continue to form new friendships over the course of their lives, whereas men tend to hold fast to old friendships, and when old friends drop away, the number of friends decreases rather than being replaced with new ones.[18] This might lead us to believe that men are more lonely than women, but the opposite is actually the case. Of course, this gender difference could always be explained by the idea that women are simply more honest than men, and tend more often to admit when asked that they are lonely.[19] However, I find such an explanation unconvincing, and it also lacks independent verification. Gender differences are applicable to many other phenomena. Women, for example, report higher levels of anxiety and depression, whereas men report higher levels of boredom. For my part, I find the most plausible explanation to be that women have different relational needs than men.

Such a gender difference in relational needs can be based in biological, psychological or social causes, and some evidence suggests that it originates in social norms rather than in biology.[20] If women have greater relational needs, it would certainly explain why women often have stronger and deeper social relationships than men but nonetheless feel more lonely. However, we have no basis for determining the cause of this difference, so let us confine ourselves to noting that studies typically demonstrate a higher prevalence of loneliness among women than men.

There are also other gender differences, such as the fact that a particularly strong loneliness predictor for men is a lack of identification with a large group or institution, for example, an organization for which one works or a university at which one studies; whereas such identification is practically irrelevant to women's experience of loneliness.[21] It can appear, furthermore, that one-on-one attachments are more important to women than to men. On the other hand, even though we see that both unmarried women and unmarried men exhibit higher levels of loneliness than do married people, the effect is greater among men than among women.[22]

Loneliness and Personality

One characteristic of being lonely or non-lonely is that the emotion tends to remain stable over a long period of time.[23] A person tested at a given time for their degree of loneliness will often score similarly on tests earlier or later in their life. Of course, changes in external circumstances influence loneliness, but for many the degree of loneliness experienced remains quite stable, despite dramatic changes in life circumstances. This suggests that loneliness for these people depends more on individual disposition than on external circumstance.

As mentioned previously, loneliness cannot be predicted by the number of people by whom an individual is surrounded, but rather by whether that person's social interactions satisfy his or her need for attachment – whether or not their social interaction is experienced as meaningful or meaningless.[24] Lonely people are no more or less physically attractive than the rest of the population, nor are they more or less intelligent. Their everyday activities are not different from those of the non-lonely. For younger people, loneliness correlates with lower alcohol consumption rates than that of their peers, but among middle-aged people, we find that loneliness correlates with higher alcohol consumption, eating more unhealthy food and doing less physical activity.[25]

Some studies conclude that lonely people have equally good social skills as non-lonely people, while other studies claim that they have weaker social skills.[26] When it comes to the Big Five in personality psychology, it appears that loneliness correlates with low scores on extraversion, agreeableness, conscientiousness and neuroticism.[27] In contrast, openness does not seem to play a role. It is well documented, furthermore, that lonely individuals have a tendency to evaluate interpersonal phenomena more negatively than do non-lonely individuals.[28] Lonely people regard both themselves and others in a more negative light than do non-lonely people.[29] A striking literary example of this is Saul Bellow's lonely protagonist Herzog, who spends much of his time mentally composing letters, which remain unsent.[30] The letters are addressed to his family, friends, celebrities and others – often after they have died, and sometimes even though he has never met them. The consistent theme of the letters is Herzog's disappointment in himself and others. One could term him a monomaniac obsessed with how everyone – himself included – falls short.

Lonely people, for their part, tend to view themselves as inferior, as less attractive and as socially incompetent. They report a greater discrepancy between who they are and who they want to be than do non-lonely people.[31] Lonely people are also perceived more negatively by others than are non-lonely people, and this effect is significantly greater among lonely people than among non-lonely[32] – that is to say, lonely people are clearly the most negative in their evaluation of other lonely people. That dramatically reduces the likelihood that two lonely individuals will come together and overcome their loneliness. Lonely people also experience their social environment as threatening to a greater extent.[33] And they consider other people to be less reliable and supportive.[34] As such, a higher degree of loneliness is correlated with individuals withdrawing into themselves in difficult situations and seeking to a lesser extent emotional support and practical help from others.[35] Lonely individuals also assist others to a lesser extent than do non-lonely people.[36] And they appear to feel less empathy for others.[37]

In conversations, lonely people tend to talk more about themselves and ask fewer questions.[38] In speed dating situations, they are seen as being less engaged and less pleasant than non-lonely individuals.[39] They seem to be difficult to get to know.[40] They are also more self-centred than others.[41] And yet, self-absorbed individuals are utterly dependent on the gaze of others. It is only by occupying another person's field of view that they find confirmation of their existence. Nonetheless, lonely people do not have a true relationship to themselves or others. They meet themselves only in the reflection they see in others' eyes. As such, other people become nothing more than a set of mirrors. The self-absorbed individual, therefore, is even lonelier than those who accept loneliness as part of their lives. The lonely individual fears the social sphere, and is also afraid of this fear. They fear that they will never master the social game, and find it difficult to rely on anyone else. Furthermore, the lonely individual regards themselves as a victim, believing that they suffer because others deny them needed recognition. Indeed, the individual reduces others first and foremost to the role of provider of such confirmation. Ultimately, they are not actually interested in others – and that is precisely the reason they are so lonely.

It is conceivable that loneliness over time generates more antisocial behaviour in a person – something that again increases loneliness, so that an internal sense of disappointing social relationships becomes, over time, an objective reality. In relationships, lonely individuals are more likely to doubt that their partner's compliments are honest, and to believe that their partner is holding back negative feelings.[42] In contrast to non-lonely individuals, they see their friends as being more dissimilar from themselves.[43] Interpreting oneself as different, however, leads a person to regard other people more negatively. For example, it is well documented that a smile is taken as friendly when it comes from someone who is considered part of one's group, but it is often taken as more threatening when it comes from a person outside the group.[44] However, people who consider themselves different from others tend to have a greater sense of being misunderstood, and are, moreover, more likely to suffer from depression.[45] Moreover, the chronically lonely have much higher expectations of interpersonal relationships than do non-lonely people.[46] Lonely individuals report less satisfaction from positive, social experiences than do non-lonely people.[47] As I discussed in Chapter Two, lonely people tend to evince a social perfectionism, whereby they place higher demands on both themselves and others when it comes to social interactions.[48]

A good representation of a lonely personality type can be found in the novel *Bare et menneske* (Only Human, 2014) by Kristine Næss. The protagonist is an author in her fifties, Bea Britt Viker, who leads a lonely life on Oslo's west side. She is divorced from Knut, with whom she has two children, and she claims it was loneliness that drove them apart.[49] She perpetually longs to have a man in her life, and complains that she has spent her 'erotic heyday on people with serious faults and deficiencies'.[50] She dismisses previous love affairs as 'fiction' in which she let herself be tricked into overlooking the fact 'that the man in question lacked spine, judgement, or something else'.[51] She says that she has 'a sort of social life', occasionally talking to old friends on the phone or meeting them for a glass of wine, but she is not really close to any of them.[52] She is uncompromisingly self-absorbed and self-pitying, but also self-critical where these character traits are concerned.[53] Nonetheless, she is more critical of others than of herself. In Bea Britt's conception, no actual relationship amounts to what it should be. Her idea of love is that it should be *total*, but she has no notion of what this totality should look like.[54] In short, Bea Britt is alone because she is lonely, rather than lonely because she is alone.

A hypothesis in previous loneliness research was that lonely people are so because they are unable to process social information as well as non-lonely people. However, that has been disproved. In studies where both lonely and non-lonely people were asked to read a blog about a person's social life or to look at photographs of people making different facial expressions, it turned out that lonely people retained much more social information from the blog and were much more precise in identifying a person's emotions from the pictures.[55] It could, in fact, appear that lonely individuals are socially over-sensitive, and that this sensitivity hinders social participation. Lonely people also tend to be more concerned with how others perceive them. All of this obviously makes it difficult to be entirely present in a given social situation because too much reflection precludes immediacy. Lonely people hunt for signs of rejection in others, and therefore find more signs of rejection and react more strongly to such signs.[56] Innocent words and actions are often interpreted as aggressive, and this perceived aggression is met with aggression from the lonely individual's side.[57] As a result, the social sphere appears to contain immense risk, and loneliness is a safe option, even if it is painful. In this way, loneliness causes social avoidance strategies. Because lonely people are less likely to regard others as potential sources of positive relationships, they will often choose strategies that reduce the likelihood of achieving attachment to them.[58]

FOUR

Loneliness and Trust

No soul is desolate as long as there is a human being for
whom it can feel trust and reverence.

GEORGE ELIOT, *Romola*

Studies have demonstrated a clear inverse correlation
between loneliness and generalized trust: the more trusting you are, the less lonely; and the less trusting you are, the
more lonely.[1] It is difficult to determine the nature of the
causal relation here, or if a causal relation even exists, but
there seems to be more evidence that a lower degree of trust
leads to loneliness than there is for the reverse.[2] The connection between loneliness and trust appears to be strong both on
an individual level and when we examine countries as a whole.

A comparative study in Norway and Denmark showed
that trust placed in other people was one of the key explana-
tory factors regarding the variation in the loneliness
experienced in both countries.[3] It is striking that Paul Auster,
when he describes his father's abyssal loneliness in *The Invention of Solitude*, places such great emphasis on his father's
inability to trust anyone, himself included.[4] The ability to
trust others and the ability to develop attachments are closely
related. As we saw in Chapter Three, lonely people interpret
their social environment as threatening to a greater degree.[5]
They perceive others as being less reliable and supportive
than do non-lonely individuals,[6] and regard others as being

less similar to themselves than do non-lonely individuals.[7] However, it is well-known in research on trust that similarity builds trust. We simply have an easier time trusting people who resemble – or whom we at least believe resemble – ourselves. If a person regards themselves as different from others, that will weaken the trust they can place in them.

Trust has been described in many ways: as a feeling, a perception, a belief, a relation or a behaviour. All of these descriptions capture important aspects of trust. No one can live completely without trust, and philosophers such as Thomas Aquinas and John Locke have correctly observed that human life would be impossible without trust. Georg Simmel remarks that society would simply disintegrate without the generalized trust humans beings place in each other.[8] In almost every daily situation in which you find yourself, you rely on other people; for example, you trust that they are not a suicide bomber, that a person is generally telling the truth, and so on. Without this kind of trust, you would become paralysed. A lack of trust, furthermore, prevents actions that presuppose trust. Yet mistrust is much more demanding that trust, because it is exhausting to always be on the lookout, to constantly be supervising your actions and those of others, hunting for signs that their intentions are on a collision course with your desires, and so on. It is not easy living with the attitude that Tony Montana has in the movie *Scarface* (1983): 'Who do I trust? Me!'

Cultures of Trust

The connection between trust and loneliness can be observed both on an individual and a state level. Countries whose inhabitants exhibit higher degrees of interpersonal trust are consistently those with a relatively low prevalence of loneliness. Similarly, countries with low trust levels are consistently those with high loneliness levels. That is, apparently, one of the key explanations for why the loneliness prevalence is so low in the Nordic countries and so high in countries such as Italy, Greece and Portugal. Likewise, we find extremely low trust levels and extremely high loneliness levels in the former Communist countries in Eastern Europe. I have not succeeded in finding prevalence studies exploring loneliness in West and East Germany respectively, but given that trust levels are significantly lower in areas formerly belonging to East Germany, there is reason to assume that loneliness levels are higher there as well.

In Norway and Denmark, a clear majority of citizens believe that one can rely on most people, whereas only one in ten people believes the same thing in Brazil and Turkey.[9] The Organisation for Economic Co-operation and Development's (OECD) surveys suggest that nine out of ten Norwegians and Danes have a 'high level' of trust in others, while only four in ten Greeks and Portuguese have the same.[10] It is obvious that such diverse levels of generalized trust must significantly impact people's interaction in these countries. We also find that Norway and Denmark have among the lowest figures of loneliness in Europe, whereas Greece and Portugal have among the highest. There has been little research conducted on loneliness in China, but there is reason to believe that levels are high there as well.[11] The inverse correlation between trust and loneliness shows up on both individual and national levels. Of course, there are exceptions – there always are – and perhaps the clearest example is Japan, where there are extremely high levels of both trust and loneliness.

It is often suggested that the Western world – and other parts of the world, for that matter – is experiencing a trust crisis, but not much evidence indicates a general decrease in trust levels. Of course, these levels do change over time and from sphere to sphere. For example, the financial crisis prompted a decrease in trust of financial institutions, and, in many countries, also of public authorities, but in some countries, such as Switzerland and Israel, we saw an increase in trust of authority.[12] Meanwhile, we find no basis on which to talk about a decrease in generalized trust, that is, in the trust we have towards each other as a whole, and it is this form of trust that is so significant for loneliness. Indeed, if we look at the Nordic countries, for example, generalized trust has been strongly increasing for decades, and that is from already high levels.[13] Naturally, trust is threatened – it is *always* threatened for the simple reason that trust is easy to break down and difficult to build up – but we have no reason to believe that trust is any more threatened today than earlier.

It is disputed what exactly creates high levels of trust in a country. Many factors come into play, such as a solid rule of law, a strong civil society, low corruption, cultural homogeneity, prosperity, economic equality and so on.[14] Furthermore, higher levels of education within a country are correlated with higher trust. There also seems to be a clear correlation between individualism and generalized trust, where trust levels are higher in individualistic societies than in collective ones. A weak state or one with corrupt authorities, such that one cannot rely on one's rights being protected, has an extremely destructive effect on generalized trust within that state.[15] Social segregation also has an extremely negative effect. In the Norwegian debate, it has been common to assert that higher trust levels are due to the welfare state. In one study, however, Andreas Bergh and Christian Bjørnskov convincingly argue that the reverse is in fact the case: that it is trust that has enabled the Norwegian welfare state.[16] This does not preclude the possibility that the development of a welfare state can in turn have a beneficial effect on trust levels, but it suggests that the key influence runs the opposite way. Having examined 77 countries, Bergh and Bjørnskov argue that a welfare state's extent can be predicted according to historic trust levels. They attempt to demonstrate this by, among other things, considering trust levels among the offspring of emigrants from Scandinavia to the USA from 150 and 70 years ago; they find that trust levels among those individuals is far higher than in the general U.S. population.

Totalitarian Loneliness

Hannah Arendt mentions loneliness in her analysis of political totalitarianism. Totalitarianism destroys the space between individuals in which they can interact freely. It destroys social space, and therefore also the distinction between private and public. It is an organized loneliness.[17] Arendt is correct that totalitarian regimes create loneliness in the populace, but it is difficult to grasp her explanation for why exactly this occurs. The weakness in Arendt's analysis is simply that trust is missing from her discussion, despite the fact that she does mention the importance of a relationship to 'trusting and trustworthy . . . equals'.[18]

Presumably, the least trusting society in history must be the Soviet Union in the 1930s.[19] There you basically could not trust anyone, nor could anyone could trust you.[20] No one could know who was an informant for the secret police, and even if you had done nothing wrong, there was always a looming danger of being arrested and sent to prison or a labour camp. Because citizens had to prove trustworthy to the regime, they could not trust each other.[21] During the 1930s, the purging of 'enemies' increasingly ran out of control, and to create the appearance of order, quotas of alleged 'traitors' were established that had to be filled, though it actually was completely unpredictable who would fit those quotas from one week to the next – it could be enough, for example, to be a philatelist. In that society, it was crucial not to reveal too much about yourself to others. Extreme caution was called for when it came to word choice, even in seemingly harmless situations, and how one expressed one's feelings. The safest approach was simply to minimize personal contact.

A strong rule of law is an essential prerequisite for trust in modern societies. Arendt underscores this in a note from 3 September 1951:

> Politics exists in order to guarantee a minimum of trust. The law that states: when you do this and that, this and that will happen; the agreement that states: when you fulfil this and that, I will fulfil this and that – these create a framework of predictability amid the unpredictable. Morality does the same. Politics and constitutions, therefore, become even more inexorable the less one can rely on morality – that is, in eras characterized by an expanding world where different moralities are relativized by their collision.[22]

Unfortunately, Arendt did not draw this point into her analysis of loneliness in a totalitarian society, and this makes it difficult to see, in the context of such analysis, why totalitarianism produces loneliness.

Indeed, it should be mentioned that Arendt continues her analysis from *The Origins of Totalitarianism* (1951) to *The Human Condition* (1958), and she asserts in the latter work that the same loneliness that characterizes totalitarian societies also makes itself generally felt in modern mass societies, where loneliness 'has assumed its most extreme and most antihuman form', on account of the breakdown in the distinction between private and public.[23] At this point, Arendt makes a mistake in her diagnosis, which she furthermore supports with nothing more than a reference to *The Lonely Crowd* (1950) by David Riesman, Nathan Glazer and Reuel Denney. She is correct that modern mass societies are characterized by a breakdown in distinction between private and public, but that breakdown is of an entirely different type from what is found in totalitarian societies, because it does not simultaneously imply that the space for free interaction between individuals is closed. This in turn has consequences for people's trust of others, which also has consequences for loneliness. When it comes to trust and interpersonal relationships, there are significant differences between democracies and totalitarian or authoritarian societies. Indeed, Aristotle already anticipates this point when he observes that friendship only exists to a small degree in tyrannies and to a larger degree in democracies.[24]

Trust in Interpersonal Interaction

It is not difficult to see why trust plays such a decisive role in the loneliness problematic. Lack of trust produces a caution that undermines the immediacy that is so important in our attachment to others. As we find in George Eliot's *Middlemarch*: 'He distrusted her affection; and what loneliness is more lonely than distrust?'[25] Mistrust isolates you completely.

When you demonstrate trust in someone, you become vulnerable, and when you demonstrate trust regarding something or someone important to you, you become extremely vulnerable. If you confide in them, you lose control over that information. If you attempt to form ties to them, you run the risk of rejection. Therefore it can be tempting to dismiss trusting people as naive. However, good evidence suggests that trusting people actually have a more accurate assessment of other people's personalities and intentions.[26] They are also more nuanced in that assessment, and they react quicker, so that interactions with others proceed more smoothly.

Trust solves a problem regarding interpersonal uncertainty. There are always risks involved in interaction with others. You can never know exactly what a person is thinking or what they might do. Strictly speaking, of course, you can never be sure what you yourself are thinking and might do either, but that is a separate issue. In close friendships and family relationships, you will overlook this risk. Indeed, a friendship cannot be real if you do not overlook this risk. Of course, one does not need to trust a particular individual in every respect: I can, for example, trust a friend to babysit my child without relying on him to also perform brain surgery on me. Some generalized trust must exist, however, and a generalized mistrust is a violation of the norm for friendship. Therefore, what La Rochefoucauld writes is accurate: 'It is more shameful to mistrust our friends than to be deceived by them.'[27] Mistrust shows that you are not a true friend, and if you are not a true friend, you might deserve to be let down: 'Our own mistrust justifies other people's deceptions.'[28]

In Francis Fukuyama's words, we can say that mistrust increases the 'transaction costs' in human interaction.[29] That makes being together more difficult. Of course, we all show each other trust, since it is impossible to live entirely without it. Yet trust comes in degrees and varieties. Therefore, it is also misleading when the Danish philosopher and theologian K. E. Løgstrup basically describes the matter as a clear dichotomy in *The Ethical Demand* (1956):

> It is characteristic of human life that we normally encounter one another with natural trust. This is true not only in case of persons who are well acquainted with one another but also in the case of complete strangers. Only because of some special circumstance doe we ever distrust a stranger in advance . . . Initially we believe one another's word; initially we trust one another. This may indeed seem strange, but it is a part of what it means to be human. Human life could hardly exist if it were otherwise. We would simply not be able to live; our life would be impaired and wither away if we were in advance to distrust one another, if we were to suspect the other of thievery and false-hood from the very outset . . . To trust, however, is to lay oneself open.[30]

Løgstrup emphasizes trust as a basic characteristic of human existence. And that is certainly accurate. Without an innate trust, we would not be able to grow up. However, we are not all trusting to the same extent, and mistrust need not be tied to the belief that another will betray us, but rather perhaps only to the idea that another person will not necessarily like or accept us. Humans with low generalized trust do not necessarily view others as malicious, but rather as *risky* – as people who *could* hurt them. Untrusting individuals are less likely to reveal personal information because they fear the response will be negative or that others could spread that information further. This hypothesis, meanwhile, distinguishes itself from the hypothesis that lonely people lack social skills.

Fear and mistrust also become self-perpetuating. Mistrust fosters more mistrust, because, among other reasons, it isolates individuals from situations where they could have learned to trust others. Lonely people perceive their social surroundings as threatening to a greater extent than do non-lonely people,[31] and this fear hinders the precise thing that could cause it to decrease: human contact. Social fear undermines immediacy regarding other people, thereby undermining social relationships. Does low trust produce greater loneliness or the reverse? Or are they mutually reinforcing? The matter is difficult to determine, but there seems to be more support for the hypothesis that low trust levels produce loneliness than the reverse.[32] One study of American students showed that those who were taught that they should not trust strangers experienced higher levels of loneliness as adults, and this effect was stronger among women than men.[33]

A considered trust is always associated with a consciousness of risk, and it contains a kernel of mistrust. It is limited and contingent: considered trust is possible only when those who demonstrate it are willing to accept that a certain risk or vulnerability exists. Yet when we show trust, we assume precisely that this exposure or vulnerability will not be exploited.

When we rely on others, we consistently interpret their words and actions in a more positive light than when we do not.[34] From a distrustful perspective, on the other hand, a person has a tendency to interpret everything in the worst light, making it difficult to enter into any relationship that might have taught the individual that people can be relied on. If you do not trust others, you will limit your interactions, and that in turn means there will be fewer chances to disprove your assumption that people are untrustworthy. Mistrust prevents you from reaching outside yourself. By shutting others out, you also shut yourself inside. And loneliness will most likely accompany you there.

FIVE

Loneliness, Friendship and Love

Sometimes you get so lonely
Sometimes you get nowhere
I've lived all over the world
I've left every place
Please be mine
Share my life
Stay with me
Be my wife

DAVID BOWIE,
'Be My Wife', *Low* (1977)

Only a person who can exhibit friendship and love can feel lonely. On the other hand, it is also reasonable to say that only a being with the capacity for loneliness can love or be someone's friend.

Loneliness inhabits every social space. Even though you share an experience with others, there are sides of that experience that belong solely to you and that you will never be able to fully convey. If you are despairing, you can always say *that* you are despairing, but just *how* despair *feels* is something you can never fully communicate. If you have an earache, you can tell others about it, and if they have also had earaches, they will know what it means and will be able to empathize with you; nonetheless, they will not be able to *share* your earache experience. Such experiences show us that there is an insurmountable distance between ourselves and others.

I will not suggest here that we necessarily know ourselves more thoroughly than we know others, because after all we are astonishingly skilled at self-deception. For example, seldom do we lie so convincingly as when we are trying to be completely honest with ourselves. However, at least we know ourselves in a different way to the ways we know others. We can escape others, by physically leaving them or by mentally shutting them out, but we cannot escape ourselves – at least not for more than brief periods, such as when we are completely consumed by play or work. You have a relationship to yourself that you do not have to others. And a significant portion of self-consciousness comes from being aware of oneself as separate from others.

However, what makes love and close friendship so fantastic is precisely the relationship to *another*, to someone who is distinct from oneself and who is not simply a copy or a shadow of oneself but someone who expands the self and provides a glimpse of the self from the outside, thereby providing a validation one could never get from oneself. The fact that another person is simply that, an *other*, is what enables such bonds.

Both friendship and love have their own, at times complicated, histories, to which I cannot do justice here.[1] Instead, I must be content with highlighting some central conceptions of the nature of friendship and love, and attempt to say something about the implications these have for loneliness. Furthermore, until the 1800s, friendship was commonly regarded as the closest personal connection a person could have, but thereafter marriage assumed that role.

On Friendship

Philosophers have written less about friendship than love, and they have written more soberly on the matter. All philosophy introduces a kind of idealization of its object, where the attempt is made to present that object as clearly as possible, since the goal is to capture that object's essence. This means that love, for its part, has assumed a form absolutely unattainable in this world. Friendship, on the other hand, tends to be presented in a more worldly fashion. The two foremost philosophers on friendship are probably Aristotle and Kant, and they discuss friendship in very different ways (something that is hardly surprising considering that they lived in societies with extremely different social relationships).

As Aristotle writes in the first book of *Politics*: 'That man is much more a political animal than any kind of bee or any herd animal is clear. For, as we assert, nature does nothing in vain; and man alone among the animals has speech.'[2] Mankind's character as a 'political animal', an animal who lives together with others of the same kind in a society, is, for Aristotle, inextricably connected to our speech ability. We need to exist in a communicative relationship with each other. More than any other creature, furthermore, human beings are developed to exist together, so that those who desire self-sufficiency and have no need of others are not human at all, but 'either a beast or a god'.[3] He further describes having a friend as 'the greatest of external goods'.[4]

Aristotle distinguishes among three types of friendship. In every form 'there is a corresponding and mutual affection that does not go unrecognized, and those who love each other wish good things to each other in that respect in which they love one another.'[5] Friendships of utility, however, are defined according to mutual advantage. Aristotle points out that friendships of utility are easily formed, and can unfortunately be confused with deeper friendship. Friendships of utility, furthermore, do not last, because the advantage on which the friendship is based can change due to shifts in life circumstances. At that point, the friendship collapses because it was not anchored in personal characteristics, but rather in something completely exterior. Next comes a friendship of pleasure, where one finds the other's society comfortable, and the friends can, for example, have a good time together. Aristotle emphasizes that this friendship is also easy to form, but remains fragile, because pleasures can also shift. These two forms of friendship, moreover, are incomplete. In contrast, he describes the friendship of virtue as complete:

> Complete friendship is that of good people, those who are alike in their virtue: they each alike wish good things to each other in so far as they are good, and they are good in themselves. Those who wish good things to a friend for his own sake are friends most of all, since they are disposed in this way towards each other because of what they are, not for any incidental reason. So their friendship lasts as long as they are good, and virtue is an enduring thing.[6]

The best friendship is the friendship of virtue among equals who wish one another well and who admire each other's virtue. This type of friendship is also more enduring, because it is anchored in who the friends are as people, deep in their very character, and the friendship therefore remains unsubjected to shifts with respect to advantage or pleasure. Aristotle, however, believes that such friendships are rare, simply because there are not many people who retain the virtue this friendship demands.[7] Such a friend is like 'another self'.[8] If one has such a friend, one will spend as much time with that person as possible, and that also means that one cannot maintain many such friendships, because the friendship more or less demands that a person devote their life to it.

Kant, for his part, describes friendship as the highest form of reciprocal love.[9] He briefly discusses two inferior forms of friendship: the friendship of need and the friendship of taste. These correspond to great extent to the Aristotelian friendships of utility and pleasure, and shall not be discussed further here. Kant then distinguishes between two types of valuable friendship, where the first is, in practice, unattainable, and the second extremely difficult to attain. The unattainable friendship creates equality among two people through mutual love and respect.[10] The reason he gives for this friendship being in practice unattainable is that one can never be certain that the relationship is indeed reciprocal, so it will always be threatened by a potential imbalance among friends. The second type of friendship consists in the complete trust two people have in revealing their thoughts, secrets and feelings to each other.[11] A person does not want to be 'alone with his thoughts', as Kant writes. However, it is risky to reveal what one thinks and feels about political matters, religion or other people. Therefore, a person desires a close confidant with whom he or she can converse without fearing betrayal. Therefore, trust is a central phenomenon in this friendship.[12] Openheartedness, moreover, is the friendship's existential basis.[13] Friends must be open to each other's thoughts and feelings, and remain sympathetic to each other, but one friend can criticize another if he believes the other to be on the wrong track. To be corrected by a friend is certainly an important part of friendship's function, but it is the ability to open oneself that is most essential. In this context, one can always ask why Kant believes this form of friendship to be more attainable than the other, since reciprocality in the relationship is also not guaranteed, but Kant provides no answer. It is clear, however, that one can have only a few good friends, since having more friends reduces the value of the single friendship.[14] In contrast to the Aristotelian friendship of virtue, the Kantian friendship of intimacy does not require that one necessarily spend so much time together. The presence of mutual trust allows the friendship to be maintained over long periods of absence. That friendship itself is limited, since one does not do much together, such as go to concerts or play tennis. Indeed, these friends do not even need to share interests. The Kantian friendship is also not utility-based, and Kant claims that it is better to bear one's burdens alone than to load them onto one's friends.[15] In so doing, we threaten to undermine the friendship, and demean the friendship of intimacy to a friendship of need. That being said, friends should also be ready to provide each other with all the help that might be required.[16]

Friendship for Kant is the solution to the loneliness that results from our 'unsocial sociability'. In *Anthropology from a Pragmatic Point of View* he writes that, instead of a social animal, it seems more plausible to regard man as 'a solitary one who shies away from his neighbors'.[17] At the same time, man is subject to the 'necessity to be a member of some civil society or other'.[18] Kant makes an important point by underscoring a duality in us, where we are both pulled towards others and pulled towards being alone:

> By antagonism, I mean in this context the unsocial sociability of men, that is, their tendency to come together in society, coupled, however, with a continual resistance which constantly threatens to break this society up. This propensity is obviously rooted in human nature. Man has an inclination to live in society, since he feels in this state more like a man, that is, he feels able to develop his natural capacities. But he also has a great tendency to live as an individual, to isolate himself, since he also encounters in himself the unsocial characteristic of wanting to direct everything in accordance with his own ideas. He therefore expects resistance all around, just as he knows of himself that he is in turn inclined to offer resistance to others.[19]

Kant points out that we need to mean something to others, to show that we have a value and to enjoy recognition.[20] In his 'unsocial sociability', a person feels impelled to show others who they are, even their innermost thoughts and feelings.[21] In the social state, people also feel a need to reveal their innermost person to someone, but since that action is also bound up with risk, a person will try to attach themselves to one person, or at most a specially chosen few, in friendship.[22] As Kant remarks in one lecture, without a friend, a person is completely isolated.[23]

If we turn to Montaigne, we find that although he prizes loneliness,[24] he prizes friendship even more, describing it as 'the most supreme point of [society's] perfection'.[25] The exemplary friendship is the friendship he has with Étienne de La Boétie, which is described as something completely different from what normally goes under the name of friendship:

> For the rest, what we commonly call friends and friendship, are nothing but acquaintance and familiarities, either occasionally contracted, or upon some design, by means of which there happens some little intercourse betwixt our souls. But in the friendship I speak of, they mix and work themselves into one piece, with so universal a mixture, that there is no more sign of the seam by which they were first conjoined.[26]

This description of their friendship is very close to the description of love given in Aristophanes' speech in Plato's *Symposium*, where two souls are created to meet and combine in a perfect unity. Montaigne describes how they 'sought one another long before we met', how they regarded each other with 'so ardent an affection' and how 'with the like affection laid open the very bottom of our hearts to one another's view'. [27] It is, furthermore, a perfect friendship, where every characteristic one might value among a variety of friends are collected into a single person, and therefore there is no room for friends other than the one.[28] Therefore it was especially crushing for Montaigne when his friend died, and he writes, 'I am no more than half of myself.'[29] Here it is a modern form of friendship Montaigne is describing, one for which emotional intimacy is fundamental – an idea Aristotle would have considered completely foreign. However, one can also ask if the friendship Montaigne is describing was not in reality a romantic relationship.

The Aristotelian friendship of virtue and Montaigne's ideal friendship are both all-consuming, and seem incompatible with having something in life besides one's friend, for example, a job or a family. The Kantian friendship of intimacy, on the other hand, is perhaps a little too limiting. Is not a friendship typically about something more than sharing thoughts and emotions not meant for the broader public? Friends usually have one or more common interest – something such as sport, or a form of cultural expression. That is to say, there is generally some third component in the friendship's structure, and that third element helps bind friends together. One can ask, of course, whether or not this fact actually makes a friendship more vulnerable, for it is reasonable to expect one of the friends to lose interest in that sport or cultural form. That being the case, however, it can also be argued that this third element would help to create a certain permanence, where an individual would continue to have that common interest, even if many other life circumstances changed.

When it comes to friendship, however, a certain amount of unselfishness must be involved.[30] A true friendship or love demands that you, in Aristotle's words, desire to do what is good for others with respect to the other, and not to yourself. And in order for the relationship to be genuine, reciprocity is required, such that the other also has the desire to do what is good for you with respect to you, and not to themselves. Friendship, furthermore, involves an objectivity that does not exist in the same way in love. We have no trouble imagining unrequited love – most of us have been in the situation where we have loved someone who has not loved us back – but unrequited friendship is more difficult to imagine. A person can love another, and the fact that the object does not return that love does not make the love illusory. A friendship without reciprocity, however, is no friendship at all.

According to Simmel, modern individualization leads to a differentiation of friendship, whereby a person no longer has one or two friends that cover the entire register, but rather a variety of friends for different needs and purposes.[31] Still, there is not much to indicate that friendship today is substantially more divided than it was in the past. In modern marriage and cohabitation relationships, however, we also find the development in which the relationship to the partner displaces other social relationships – the thought being that one's life partner should cover all one's social requirements. Love places even greater demands on identity sharing than does friendship. Very few people find it problematic that their friends have other friends, but very few people find it acceptable for their love to love someone else. Friendship demands part of you; love tends to demand all of you.

On Love

Love presupposes independent, separate individuals, and it tries to overcome this separation. In Plato's *Symposium*, Aristophanes gives a speech explaining how mankind originally consisted of androgynous beings, each composed of a man and a woman with two faces, four arms and four legs.[32] However, that being was so powerful that it posed a threat to the gods, and therefore Zeus chose to sunder the creature in two.

> When its nature was cut in two, each – desiring its
> own half – came together; and throwing their arms
> around one another and entangling themselves with

one another in their desire to grow together, they began to die off due to hunger and the rest of their inactivity, because they were unwilling to do anything apart from one another; and whenever one of the halves did die and the other was left, the one that was left tried to seek out another and entangle itself with that . . .[33]

This original ideal state, where two were inextricably one, is what we all seek, Aristophanes says, and only when we succeed in reaching such unity will we truly be happy. However, he also realizes that this ideal is unattainable, and suggests, therefore, that we must instead hunt for 'that which is closest to it' and strive to 'get a favorite whose nature is to one's taste'.[34] Aristophanes' speech is based on the idea that human nature as such is incomplete. We must attach ourselves to someone because we are deficient in ourselves. Despite the rather ridiculous image of a being with two faces, four legs and four arms, we intuitively grasp Aristophanes' point: when you love another and are loved in turn, you feel *whole*, as if you and your beloved formed a perfect unity. There is a conviction that love can overcome the loneliness every human being feels. This love, which exists, exceeds every other emotion, and gives us a sense of belonging that surpasses anything we have ever known. It is like an intoxication, but it is an intoxication that brings with it the sense of actual *meaning*, the meaning for which all other forms of intoxication are only pale substitutes.

One important feature of Aristophanes' speech is that there is one person that is right for each and every one of us, and if we can only succeed in finding that individual, all our problems will essentially vanish like dew before the sun: then you will have found the person who fulfils you and gives your life the meaning it has lacked. The problem with the picture Aristophanes paints is that it imposes an impossible burden on the beloved, and on the relationship as a whole. To expect from another person that he or she will make you *whole* and will form a seamless unity with yourself is to place that person in a hopeless position. From that perspective, it impossible for the other person to do anything but 'fail'. The other will always maintain their separation, will always be an *other*, even if a person intoxicated by love can trick themselves into over-looking that fact. It cannot be another person's responsibility to ensure that your life has the prerequisite meaning. Another essential problem with this idea is that it in fact places love beyond reach, because you will also never succeed in finding a person with whom you are in total harmony.

You might tell yourself until your dying day that 'I'm capable of love, but have just never found the right person,' because you demand such exact compliance with your idea of who that person should be, with some endless list of 'demand specifications', from which is permitted no deviation, that you will never meet a real person that lives up to your standards. However, if you live your life without finding a person to love – not because you are excluded, isolated or rejected but because no real person you come in contact with can live up to your standards – a more accurate conclusion is that you are actually not capable of loving anyone because your own conception of love precludes actual love in your life.

Aristophanes' speech becomes, long before Romanticism emerged, the embodiment of Romantic love. It is a form of love we find again in the correspondence between Abélard and Héloïse – especially in the letters from Héloïse – after Abélard is castrated by Héloïse's relations and she becomes a nun and spends the rest of her life in a cloister. Reading her letters, it is striking how all-consuming this love is, so all-consuming that God himself is not present in them because Abélard entirely fills her consciousness.[35] In Romantic love, the beloved assumes divine proportions. One might ask how far the relationship would have gone if it had not been halted by Héloïse's relatives – if the couple had in fact spent their whole lives together. It is doubtful that Abélard would have maintained his sheen of divinity in solid, everyday life.

Goethe's Werther disseminates an idea of love even more pumped up on emotional steroids. In the introduction to the work, Werther writes about the pleasure he takes in his freedom and solitude.[36] He finds his world within.[37] Then he meets Charlotte, and falls insanely in love. He incessantly longs to be with her and becomes ecstatic at her least touch or word. He is also plagued by gruesome doubts as to whether or not she loves him. Such doubt becomes even more difficult to bear because he regards love as the only true source of meaning in existence. Unsurprisingly, his love for Lotte is doomed at the outset. No matter how wildly enamoured he is, he simply cannot transcend himself. He is expressively incompetent in both art and love, and he realizes this when he says: 'my heart is mine and mine alone.'[38] He does not function well with other people, with whom he is always decisively finding fault. Aside from Lotte, of course, whom he idealizes and who is 'divine'.[39] Ultimately, he cannot comprehend that she has actually married another, that she loves anyone besides himself.[40] Even in his love for Lotte, Werther is essentially unable to break free of his self-absorption – the only thing that matters is his own subjectivity. It all ends, as is well known, in suicide, when that subjectivity collides with the reality that Lotte does not want him. It is crucial for the story of Werther's boundless devotion to Lotte – which in reality is simply a devotion to his own infatuation – that the relationship never be fulfilled. Even if Werther had not taken his own life, the love between them would never have been consummated, would never have resulted in a long coexistence, because she simply desires another. The relationship can never become a reality, and so Werther's desire will never succumb to a banal and boring everyday life.

When it comes to the famous love stories, it is striking how few of them concern lifelong love; rather, they describe

love's first intoxication. How would Romeo and Juliet's existence have looked if they had survived, got married and become
middle-aged? Would it have been possible to maintain the same
passion? They die after a single night together, and therefore
that question does not enter into the play's framework. The
same with the movie *Titanic*. If the ship had never collided with
the iceberg, but instead made it safe and sound from South-
ampton to New York, how would the story of upper-class Rose
and penniless Jack have gone? Or if not only Rose, but Jack
as well, was saved? Because their relationship is so fleeting,
moreover, everyday concerns do not make themselves felt, such
as the fact that one might have quirks that irritate the other,
from foul-smelling socks to one liking seafood while the other
cannot stand it. Falling in love is an important part of love, but
it is nonetheless only one part. Not that falling in love blinds
you; as Heidegger observes, love also enables us to *see* things
we cannot otherwise see when we are not in love.[41] However,
we can also say that falling in love is rather single-focused and
one-dimensional, because, at that point, a person still only
knows and is concerned with a few aspects of their chosen one.
Love itself unfolds over a longer period of time, during which
our perception of the other person takes on an entirely different
complexity. The most famous love stories limit themselves to a
tiny slice of love, to its beginning, to before it starts or right as it
is starting. Yet falling in love becomes the romantic perspective
on love's essence. These stories might provide a good picture of
how love begins, but not how it unfolds.

Cynicism and Scepticism

The opposite of love's extreme idealization is the cynicism
that we see, for example, in Don Draper when, in the first
episode of *Mad Men*, he tells a lover: 'What you call love was
invented by guys like me, to sell nylons. You're born alone
and you die alone and this world just drops a bunch of rules

on top of you to make you forget those facts.' Such cynicism is also brilliantly expressed in the Pet Shop Boys' pop song 'Love is a Bourgeois Construct':

> When you walked out you did me a favour
> you made me see reality
> that love is a bourgeois construct
> It's a blatant fallacy
> You won't see me with a bunch of roses
> promising fidelity
> Love doesn't mean a thing to me

However, the cynic in this song is not a true cynic. He tries to tell himself this in order to overcome the despair at having been left by his lover. If love were just an illusion, or rather, a bourgeois construct, his loss would not be so crushing. However, as he also admits in the song, he will maintain this perspective on love only 'until you come back to me'.

Cynics believe that love as such is impossible, that it is only an illusion that serves a purpose. A sceptic on love does not necessarily dismiss love as impossible, but for sceptics love is always weighted with doubt. A love sceptic is someone who is unable to convince themselves that he or she can be loved in a true way.[42] Or that anyone can really love another because there is no way for two souls to actually meet. In Dryden's translation of Lucretius, we find:

> They gripe, they squeeze, their humid tongues
>   they dart,
> As each would force their way to t' other's heart:
> In vain they only cruize about the coast;
> For bodies cannot pierce, nor be in bodies lost;
> . . .
> All ways they try, successless all they prove,
> To cure the secret sore of ling'ring love.

W. B. Yeats proclaimed these lines to be the best description of sex in existence, and stated that 'the tragedy of sexual intercourse is the perpetual virginity of the soul.'[43]

None of us are safe from experiencing a similar scepticism, either as the one who doubts or the one who is doubted. Scepticism does not have to imply the suspicion that a person has somehow been betrayed or that the other is dishonest, but can just as well be a lack of trust that real love is even possible, despite the fact that the other person's intentions are entirely positive. Think of Gabriel, the protagonist in James Joyce's short story 'The Dead', when his wife Gretta is moved to tears by thoughts of a song. He asks her why she is crying, and she says that one time, long before the two of them met, she loved a boy who used to sing that song. The boy died when he was only seventeen years old, and he died for her. This comes as a shock to Gabriel: 'While he had been full of memories of their secret life together, full of tenderness and joy and desire, she had been comparing him in her mind with another.'[44] In a single blow he goes from believing he was her one and only to being a ridiculous figure in his own eyes for having held such a belief. Gabriel questions if Gretta ever truly loved him, and if she has not remained with him simply out of duty; he suspects that she has always harboured a longing for the boy who died – that *he* was her real love. This expectation, that one person must be everything for the other, that two people can enter a seamless unity, makes love impossible. After all, the other person had a life before you met, a life that will not simply meld with yours without a trace of its past existence, and they have thoughts and emotions in which you can never fully participate. These facts must simply be accepted.

Charles Baudelaire and Agnar Mykle, among others, provide more examples of the collapse in understanding that surrounds the idea of becoming one. Baudelaire addresses this subject in a prose poem, 'The Eyes of the Poor', in which the narrator and a woman sit in a café, having 'assured each other that our thoughts were thoughts in common and that our two souls would be one'. Outside on the street before them is a poor man in his forties with his two children. The narrator is gripped by the eyes of the poor family, which gleam with joy and admiration, and he feels shame at his own abundance compared with the poor family's living conditions. As he turns to the woman, expecting to find his own thoughts mirrored in her, she exclaims: 'I find these people insupportable, their eyes wide as barn doors! Couldn't you ask the waiter to get them out of here?' The narrator concludes that one can never really know another person.[45] In Agnar Mykle's short story 'Stjernene' (Stars), a man who is about to kill some kittens experiences gruesome torments. The thing that disturbs him most, however, is the equanimity, almost indifference, his wife shows:

> He looked at his wife, stunned. He had to grasp his stomach in horror. What manner of creature was a woman? What manner of a creature was she? Here he had been thinking for years, for twelve years, that she was the world's sweetest and most thoughtful person, and yet she had no more compassion in her than in a butcher![46]

From this perspective, the story continues the subject of Mykle's novel *The Song of the Red Ruby*, where Ask Burlefot draws the conclusion that 'love is a lonely thing.' This loneliness emerges when you realize that the person with whom you thought you were forming a unity is, in reality, different from what you believed, when the unity collapses and you are separated by an abyss.

In Leo Tolstoy's short story 'Family Happiness' (1859), furthermore, we follow a story about the middle-aged Sergey and a younger woman, Masha, that takes place from her perspective. Gradually she falls in love with him, and she feels that the two of them really are one. During their honeymoon, she describes their meals together, which are full of laughter and confidences, but after only two months she experiences loneliness in the relationship, because there seems to be a compartment of his mind that is closed to her.[47] Masha also begins to feel stultified, and says that everyday love is insufficient compared to the ecstasy of falling in love. In order to remedy the boredom, she casts herself into high society, but is bored by the tea and dinner parties. After that their mutual dissatisfaction with each other grows, and they begin to lead entirely separate lives, even though they live beneath the same roof. Having two children together, moreover, does not create a greater closeness between them.

The change comes when they travel to Masha's childhood home, where their romance started, and she begins to reflect on how the whole thing developed. She thinks that love is dead, and that they are both to blame for killing it. When she tells Sergey these thoughts, he answers that the old love has to die in order to clear the way for something new, and that there is no reason to blame either of them for this happening because in a certain sense it was unavoidable. This precise realization is what brings them together again, and a new love grows, which, however, is different from first falling in love. Without making Tolstoy's short story a norm for every relationship – after all, it ends in what the contemporary reader would consider an excessively dispassionate, 'mature' love – it does contain some insights that are valid for every relationship. Like *Romeo and Juliet* and other similar stories, it provides a credible picture of falling in love. However, because Masha and Sergey's relationship turns realistic and extends beyond the single night Romeo and Juliet had together, it remains true to love's realities and not just its idealizations. In order for love to exist, a new foundation must be built over time.

Love, Friendship and Identity

When you fall in love, you feel a complete unity, but it is a unity with someone whom you do not entirely know and who does not entirely know you. As the relationship develops over time, you will find that the other person is different from what you first thought, and the other person will discover the same about you. Of course, you will also find that you have unexpected things in common, because there were sides of yourselves you did not previously show, and this confirms your original harmony. More distressing, however, are all those characteristics that break with the harmony; with the Platonic, seamless unity. On the other hand, Platonic unity is a fictional entity. Real love is a coexistence, a unity of two, to be sure, but one that is in no way seamless and that is also capable of containing difference. The fact is, every relationship will contain pain and disappointments that must be overcome if the love is to continue. The question is whether such difficulties are to be regarded as signs that love is past or as a basis for a further deepening of that love. Unity in love will always contain two lonelinesses. You can always leave the relationship when the fictional unity of falling in love ebbs or collides with reality, in order to seek a new falling in love, which will in turn also be replaced by a new love. It is, however, an existence where no one can every really know you and where you can never really know anyone else. A less lonely option would seem to contain the recognition that the Platonic unity must give way to something else, and that while that something else may hold loneliness, it also provides a place for two lonelinesses to meet.

We are cognizant of the significance friendship and love have to human life, for overcoming the loneliness with which we all are essentially threatened, but we must also keep in mind that neither of these can be perfectly realized. Neither friendship nor love is served by a social perfectionism that hardly allows room for departure from an ideal conception before that relationship is perceived as being tenuous. However, it is precisely this social perfectionism that, as mentioned, is more common among lonely individuals than non-lonely. The lonely person thinks that they are unloved and that no one will befriend them, but perhaps the problem is rather that, because they place such impossible demands on friendship and love, they are not capable of loving or befriending someone.

You require friendship and love in your life. You need to care about someone, and to have someone care about you. Caring about someone gives the world its meaning. It is through such caring that you constitute yourself as a person.[48] You *are* what you care about. If you do not care about anything, you are nothing. If you only care about yourself, you are caught in a rather empty loop. You need to be needed. You require recognition from someone whom you can recognize as an equal.

Your self-identity is not anchored deep within yourself, detached from others, but is rather anchored in your attachment to others. That is why it is so damaging to self-identity when attachment to others proves unsuccessful. Without some attachment to others, you are an inferior version of yourself, simply because central parts of yourself remain fallow. Ultimately, there is only one answer to the question of why I should be friends with *x* and in a love relationship with *y*, and that is that *x* and *y* make me a better version of myself than I would otherwise be. As such, one can claim that egotistical motives always accompany friendship and love, but at the same time it must be acknowledged that a part of 'the best' of you is the ability to both desire and do the best for others without thinking of your own gain. Both friendship and love presuppose a shared identity. A large part of the answer to the question of who I am is that I am friends with *x* and in a love relationship with *y*. When I think about myself, my 'I' also contains an 'us'. That also means that love and friendship take us in a different direction than does individuality.

Central to Karl Jaspers's philosophy is loneliness. He writes, "To be an "I" means to be solitary."[49] Whoever says 'I' establishes a distance, draws a circle around themselves. The work of loneliness is the work of the I. Loneliness can only exist where there are individuals. However, where there are individuals, there is both the desire for individuality (and the attendant craving for solitude) and the affliction of individuality (and the attendant craving to emerge from loneliness).[50] Human beings harbour an inner contradiction whereby they wish both to be left in peace and to share a deep belonging with others. Loneliness for Jaspers is inextricably bound with the *consciousness* of being separate from others, and that, in turn, is inextricably connected to our communicative faculties. Only those who, via loneliness, have become an I can communicate, and those who lack the communicative ability cannot be lonely or even be an I.[51] The task all people are forced to accomplish, therefore, is to overcome loneliness through communication without losing themselves. Human communication, that is, often has the character of being a 'hopeless attempt at community among the lonely'.[52] For Jaspers there is only one true experience in which both individuality and belonging can coexist, and that is in love between two equal partners who can communicate on the same level. Meanwhile, he observes such love is extremely rare – that it is more ideal than actual.

If Jaspers thinks that love can function as a definitive cure for loneliness, we can agree that such love has a more ideal character than something recognizable from the real world. However, there is a love that is not so rare and that for the most part eradicates loneliness, even if those who love do occasionally feel lonely. This love, however, has no guarantees. Even though you feel so deep a sense of belonging with another person that you cannot imagine ever feeling different, a relationship is always in motion because the people in it are always in motion. And even if you feel an extremely deep belonging with another, there will always be a distance and a loneliness there that must be respected.

Idealized stories about the nature of love lead us astray, and make it more difficult to realize that love that is most certainly real, no matter what love cynics and love sceptics claim. If you establish an ideal of love that no one will ever be able to meet, however, you thereby make it impossible to ever have your need for love satisfied. You simply guarantee yourself a lonely existence. And Don Draper and other cynics are correct: we are all relegated to a type of loneliness throughout our lives, but that loneliness can meet other lonelinesses – and then you are no longer so lonely. It is, in Rilke's words, possible to attain 'a love which consists in the mutual guarding, bordering and saluting of two solitudes'.[53]

SIX

Individualism and Loneliness

The ebbing of community over the last several decades has been silent and deceptive. We notice its effects in the strained interstices of our private lives and in the degradation of our public life, but the most serious consequences are reminiscent of the old parlor puzzle: 'What's missing from this picture?' Weakened social capital is manifest in the things that have vanished almost unnoticed – neighborhood parties and get-togethers with friends, the unreflective kindness of strangers, the shared pursuit of the public good rather than a solitary quest for private goods.

ROBERT D. PUTNAM, *Bowling Alone: The Collapse and Revival of American Community*

The image contained of our contemporary society in this quotation from Robert D. Putnam in 2000 is more or less a standard narrative in newer social science: we are succumbing to a fateful undermining of community, where individualism triumphs over all, thereby transforming us into lonely hedonists and egoists. Is this narrative correct? Does loneliness particularly haunt the modern and late modern individual?

What is a Liberal Individual?

The liberal individual did not just suddenly appear at a particular time and place, but instead emerged over centuries, and is still developing. One recent development, however, is that for the first time in history the liberal individual is becoming the basic unit in social reproduction.[1] Not all people reside in liberal democracies, of course – just about half of the world's population does. And not everyone who resides in a liberal democracy embodies 'the liberal individual'. On the other hand, one can also find liberal individuals in countries that are not liberal democracies, such as China. The general tendency, however, is that the liberal individual is becoming the social and political norm, despite the fact that countless counter-examples and conflicting developmental trends do exist.

Ulrich Beck writes that 'the basic figure of *fully developed* modernity is the *single person*.'[2] Or the 'individual', if you will. The liberal individual is a historical reality. Yet why do I use the phrase *liberal* individual? Simply because that individual is concerned with or takes for granted liberal rights such as freedom of expression, right to property, privacy and so on. This basic thought is well-formulated in John Stuart Mill's Romantic liberalism, in which he imagines an inviolable circle drawn around every individual.[3]

Key to our understanding of the liberal individual's role in a society is what is often called negative liberty: the existence of a variety of possibilities, and not just those alternatives one actually prefers, but also those alternatives one would choose not to take advantage of.[4] This individual believes his freedom to be violated if he is forced to do something he would have done of his own accord anyway. Negative liberty is a rather empty freedom concept, however, since it essentially does nothing more than say that as many alternatives as possible should remain open. It does not indicate that any one form of self-realization is better, but simply establishes the broadest possible framework for self-realization, limited only by the idea that one person's negative liberty should not exist at the cost of another's. The liberal individual, meanwhile, does not desire simply what Amartya Sen calls freedom's possibility aspect, but also its process aspect.[5] Not only will the individual attempt to reach various life goals, he also wishes to evaluate the alternatives, and choose which of those to realize. As such, the individual craves a sphere of non-interference, and his choice alternatives should only be limited by another's right to the same amount of freedom. The liberal individual, furthermore, is not at all antisocial but wishes to choose with whom to socialize. The liberal individual regards him- or herself as unique, independent and self-determining, and the liberal democracy contains an immense variety of lifestyles and possibilities for autonomous choice. The liberal individual does not only desire negative liberty, but also positive liberty, which is synonymous with autonomy. Positive liberty consists in living in accordance with one's *own* values. This extends beyond non-interference and involves taking control over and shaping one's own life.

Georg Simmel makes a well-known distinction between two forms of individualism: a quantitative and a qualitative individualism, the first of which dominated in the eighteenth century and the second from 1800 onwards.[6] We could also talk about Enlightenment individualism and Romantic individualism here. The basic character of quantitative individualism, which Simmel associates with Kant in particular, is independence. The individual is conceived as being free of every normative limitation, excepting ones which are self-imposed. Simmel argues that this understanding of the individual, however, is deficient, because the only content the individual has left is that stemming from his or her own reason. As Simmel formulates it, we will then merely 'have individuality', but not be individuals.[7] As such, another concept of the individual began to emerge, one which emphasized not just the individual's quantitative separation but his qualitative differences. In my opinion, Simmel exaggerates the purely quantitative aspects of Enlightenment individualism, and there are also obvious aspects of qualitative individualism in Kant's thought, which calls for a person to develop a unique individuality for which he or she is then responsible. According to Simmel, however, the more extreme variety of qualitative individualism is developed by Nietzsche.[8] Simmel did not believe that qualitative individualism had replaced quantitative, but rather that they existed side by side because they had yet to be synthesized. He also argued that the co-existence of these two forms of individualism could be observed in the modern metropolis, whose inhabitants embody them both.[9] These city-dwellers have a significant space of freedom, separated from others by both physical and mental aspects – a fact that also created a desire to stand out as unique, to be distinguished by personal uniqueness from one's surroundings.

The individual has an extremely reflexive relationship to him- or herself. Such reflexivity obviously exists in every society, but it is significantly radicalized in societies where people are not so strongly bound by traditions that tell them who they are.[10] The individual must create a self-identity according to the resources he or she has on hand, rather than take on an identity that is given, and must therefore perpetually supervise, maintain and modify him- or herself.

The liberal individual should be someone 'special'. Individualism's appearance endows a person with a new responsibility for self-*becoming*. As Nietzsche formulated it: 'You should become who you are.'[11] Not only should you be an individual, but you should preferably be a self that has shaped itself. Obviously, that is impossible. Strictly speaking, there is no such thing as the *self-made man*. One example from the world of literature of just such a person, one who wishes to create himself from the ground up, is Dostoevsky's Underground Man.[12] He believes that freedom is only possible on the basis of complete independence from every conceivable power or force, but that is a criterion that can never be fulfilled. None of us can ever be supremely self-motivating without external influence. You will never be able to define your person completely independently of your surroundings, independent of all that shaped you before your attempt to define yourself.[13] The liberal individual has a wealth of conceptions about the world and himself. He has values and preferences. Very few of these things can be regarded as objects of explicit choice. Of course, in principle everything can be modified, but only based on other conceptions, values and preferences that are not selected. Every self-transformation has its roots in what already exists. The liberal individual is not as unfettered by others as he might like to believe.

As George Herbert Mead, among others, points out, we create ourselves through our interaction with other selves, and therefore can in principle draw no clear distinction between our own self and those of others.[14] Selfhood implies the ability to take up a position outside oneself, and to see oneself as others do. From this perspective, the self is a *social* product. We teach ourselves to perceive ourselves as others do, and we transform ourselves through our interaction with other selves. Meanwhile, the self also maintains a certain independence in connection to others.

The liberal individual is not as autonomous, socially unfettered and supremely self-motivating as he believes, but he also does not vanish without a trace into society. The liberal individual is of course socially situated, but social belonging does not answer the individual's one question: how should I live? This fact is also accepted by Communitarian philosophers such as Michael Sandel, who writes: 'As a self-interpreting being, I am able to reflect on my history and in this sense to distance myself from it.'[15] This is all the liberal individual needs in order to ascertain that the self is the ultimate judge in all normative questions. In relationship to others, the liberal individual, for his part, is caught in a paradox where he desires both unlimited freedom and authentic belonging.[16] Obviously, this desire cannot be realized, at least not so long as freedom is equated with independence or the absence of boundaries. As we shall see in what follows, however, the liberal individual seems capable of uniting freedom and belonging in practice. Until now, the individual has been painted mostly as an abstract entity. Let us now see how this figure actually materializes in the real world.

Living Solo

In 1949, the anthropologist George Peter Murdoch published a study of 250 cultures from different eras and parts of the world, and concluded that the nuclear family was a universal entity that dominated, with certain variations, in all cultures.[17] Murdoch was met with objections from some other anthropologists, who pointed to other ways of life whereby people organized themselves into different types of social unities. Both Murdoch and his critics, however, agreed that people in all times and places generally structure their lives such that they live together with others. Of course, they were also clear that hermit monks and other solo-dwellers do exist, but these tend to be exceptions inside their cultures. However, as the sociologist Eric Klinenberg observes in his book *Going Solo*, this fact is changing significantly. Among the statistics he highlights, 22 per cent of Americans in 1950 were single, and 9 per cent of households were comprised of solo-dwellers. Today 50 per cent of American adults are single, and solo-dwellers comprise 23 per cent of all households.[18] An equal percentage of households are composed of two adults with no children, and that is more common than all other living arrangements, such as the nuclear family or shared living. More women than men live alone. And women who live alone continue to a greater extent than men to live alone, though both groups, having lived alone once, are more likely to continue solo than to move in with someone.[19] A third of solo-dwellers fall into the age group of 65-plus, but the most significant increase in solo-dwellers is found in the under-35 group, where ten times as many people live alone today as in 1950. Meanwhile, we also see increasingly more elderly adults living alone. The EU estimates that one in three elderly individuals lived alone in 2010.[20] Surveys find that the most commonly given reason for this is that they prefer living alone to moving in with their children or into a senior living facility.[21] If we turn to the Nordic countries, we find the world's highest figures: 45–50 per cent are single-person households. However, this is not purely a Western phenomenon. We find the most rapid increase in the number of solo-dwellers in China, India and Brazil.[22] Globally, this development seems to be happening at an extremely quick rate, where there has been an estimated increase from 153 million single-person households in 1996 to 202 million in 2006.

In *Capitalism, Socialism and Democracy* (1943), Joseph Schumpeter argued that just such a development would take place. He wrote that family life and parental roles would mean less for people in modern, capitalistic societies, and that an increasingly larger number of individuals would choose not to make huge sacrifices in order to live in a family:

> These sacrifices do not consist only of items that come within the reach of the measuring rod of money but comprise in addition an indefinite amount of loss of comfort, of freedom from care, and opportunity to enjoy alternatives of increasing attractiveness and variety.[23]

Schumpeter's prophecy has become a social reality.

A person who chooses to live alone need not be more asocial than other people. The fact that a person lives alone obviously does not imply that the individual in question is more alone than people who live with others. We see, for example, that people who live alone have more contact with friends and relatives than is the case for those who live together with others, whereas married people spend less time with friends and relatives than they did when they were single.[24] Solo-dwellers visit friends on a weekly basis to a greater extent, are more often a part of a social group, and spend evenings with friends more often than do people who live with a partner. It is, therefore, not evident that single individuals and solo-dwellers have less social contact than those who choose to live with others. It may be that they are equally social, but simply prefer another type of sociality.[25]

It appears that today's single-dwellers have less need for attachment to others than those who live with others, and they exhibit neither lower satisfaction with existence nor a higher loneliness prevalence than those who live with others.[26] This is surprising, considering that people who live alone have typically reported higher levels of loneliness than people who live with others.[27] Most people would immediately assume that an increase in the number of solo-dwellers would be accompanied by an equal increase in the number of people who feel lonely, but that is not what empirical studies on loneliness's scope tell us. Loneliness figures appear to have changed astonishingly little during this dramatic shift in way of life.

Perhaps the reason you are alone is more important that the fact you are alone. The relationship one has to others within said aloneness can be determinate for how that condition is experienced. A person can be alone because they have chosen it or because they are socially excluded, where the former is presumably experienced as positive and the latter as painful. If the increase in the number of solo-dwellers is due to an increase in people choosing to live that way, it is only to be expected that reported loneliness does not increase. The stability in the loneliness rate would then be explained by the fact that solo-dwelling is a self-chosen way of life.

An Individual Haunted by Loneliness?

Much contemporary literature, especially of the more popular sort, gives the impression that the modern liberal individual is a tortured soul, haunted by loneliness, alienation, anxiety and depression. As an article in *The Atlantic* puts it: 'We suffer from unprecedented alienation. We have never been more detached from one another, or lonelier.'[28] There is no shortage of books that claim we are becoming increasingly isolated and lonely, and they are often widely read. Max Weber argues that individuals suffer from a vast, inner isolation, and connects this to the emergence of Protestantism.[29] Simmel, for his part, especially emphasizes the individual's loneliness in big-city life. In post-war social studies loneliness essentially comprises the 'standard diagnosis' of modern life, typically with individualism functioning as the main culprit for all manner of evils. A particularly influential work is *The Lonely Crowd* (1950) by David Riesman, Nathan Glazer and Reuel Denney. Similar books have followed in its wake, such as Vance Packard's *A Nation of Strangers* (1972) and Christopher Lasch's *The Culture of Narcissism* (1979). In 1995, Robert Putnam published his essay 'Bowling Alone', followed by a book of the same title five years later. In 2009, Jacqueline Olds and Richard S. Schwartz published *The Lonely American* and in 2011 came Sherry Turkle's *Alone Together*. The impact of these books extends far beyond academic circles into the broader public, and even though they have typically taken their data from the U.S., they are assumed to hold significant implications for the Western world as a whole.

A typical claim in social studies literature on loneliness is that loneliness is largely a result of modern individualism. This thought actually dates back to Tocqueville's study of democracy in America in the 1830s.[30] Francis Fukuyama's lament on the sorry state of contemporary society fits effortlessly into such a perspective:

The second problem with a culture of individualism is that it ends up being bereft of community. A community is not formed every time a group of people happens to interact with one another; true communities are bound together by the values, norms, and experiences their members share. The deeper and more strongly held those common values, the stronger the sense of community. The trade-off between personal freedom and community, however, does not seem obvious or necessary to many. As people have been liberated from their traditional ties to spouses, families, neighborhoods, workplaces, and churches, they have expected to retain social connectedness. But they have begun to realize that their elective affinities, which they can slide into and out of at will, have left them feeling lonely and disoriented, longing for deeper and more permanent relationships.[31]

The social studies scholar who has perhaps received the greatest attention in recent years owing to such a diagnosis is Robert Putnam, who suggests that the decline in participation in bowling leagues is symptomatic of a general erosion of social networks, something which in turn has led to the erosion of social capital. He admits that Americans have continued to join organizations and that they communicate with each other more than ever, but claims that there is a basic lack of 'real ties to real people'.[32] Putnam's essay and book received far more attention than the many studies whose findings were in conflict with Putnam's assertions.[33] When it came to the organizations Putnam studied, it is true that there was a significant decrease in membership, but there was also a corresponding membership increase in other organizations. In actuality, there has been a notable stability in organization membership. Very little can be deduced from the fact that there was a decline in the specific organizations Putnam studied, since it may simply be that these organizations are historically outdated and have been replaced by others. For the most part, newer studies of social capital in the USA find very little change at all, though some present a more mixed bag and some occasionally present an increase.[34] Only Putnam finds decrease exclusively, and he paints a gloomy picture based on his discovery: 'the degradation of our public life', 'weakened social capital' and citizens who are on 'a solitary quest for private goods'.[35]

In reality, there is little reason for accepting Putnam's conclusion. As Claude S. Fischer has demonstrated in detail, neither the quantity nor the quality of personal relationships has changed much in the USA since 1970.[36] Of course, there have been plenty of transformations, such that people to greater extent live alone, marry later, have fewer relatives and so forth, but essentially people are just as socially active as before. The number of people who claim to be socially isolated remains practically unchanged. However, Fischer does point to one significant change: even though Americans are members of just as many organizations as they typically were before, they are less active in these organizations.[37] They seem to regard membership as less binding than previously.

One widely cited article claims that the number of Americans who have no one with whom to discuss important matters has tripled between 1985 and 2004, and comprises a quarter of the population.[38] The study immediately received broad discussion in the mass media, and its figures have been cited by many other studies. However, what is rarely cited are the reservations of the authors themselves, since they express uncertainty with regards to the findings and write that the figures surrounding the scope of social isolation are probably too high. Claude Fischer has underscored that the study's findings conflict so substantially with practically all other research in the area and, furthermore, are beset by such notable methodological weaknesses that one should draw no conclusions whatsoever from the relevant changes in social networks.[39]

Furthermore, there is simply no reason to believe that increased individualism should itself promote higher levels of loneliness. There are certainly studies that suggest that individualistic societies do have higher levels of loneliness than collective societies.[40] However, most studies find the exact opposite: loneliness's prevalence is generally higher in collectivistic societies than individualistic societies.[41] South European countries such as Italy, Greece and Portugal have higher rates. Eastern European countries have higher levels than do West European.[42] Japan, which is exceedingly collectivistic, has among the world's highest levels. Additionally, it tends to be that lack of relationship to one's family proves more significant for loneliness in collectivistic societies than in individualistic ones, whereas the relationship to friends is more important in individualistic than in collectivistic societies.[43] Nonetheless, a study of 13,000 students from 31 countries did not show greater satisfaction with family relationships in collectivistic versus individualistic societies.[44] Despite its frequency, the assertion that modern individualism creates greater loneliness finds little empirical support.

The liberal individual seems to be getting along fine. For the most part, that individual does not lack a social network, but he or she also expects the impossible in terms of a combination of complete freedom and belonging. It can be tempting to suggest that the liberal individual has a shallower relationship to others, not to mention little sense of obligation, and one might expect this would imply a greater vulnerability for emotional, rather than social, loneliness, but there is little support for the claim that any increase in emotional loneliness has taken place. In terms of social loneliness, the liberal individual is undoubtedly a social creature, but at the same time wants to choose with whom to socialize. The liberal individual clearly has a narcissistic streak, but nonetheless cares about others.[45] Generally, the liberal individual is a figure who harbours many inner contradictions, but generally appears to be managing these contradictions well.

Loneliness and Social Media

Countless books and articles have warned of the serious consequences inherent in our use of social media. According to Hubert Dreyfus, the Internet will cause us to become isolated from each other, thereby undermining trust, responsibility and duty.[46] Sherry Turkle writes about how social media makes us 'alone together'.[47] The most calamitous descriptions create the impression that we are like the inhabitants of the planet Solaria in Isaac Asimov's science fiction novel *The Naked Sun* (1957). On Solaria, people live alone or at most with a spouse, and they learn from birth to avoid personal contact with others – what they call 'seeing' – and instead to prefer 'viewing', which is virtual communication through avatars.

An early study of the Internet predicted that extended Internet use would have significant adverse affects and would create greater loneliness.[48] When those same researchers conducted a follow-up study many years later, however, they determined that most of those presumed adverse effects simply had not materialized.[49] On the contrary, it emerged that higher levels of Internet usage were correlated with higher levels of subjective well-being and social interaction. This finding has also been corroborated by other studies.[50] Empirical studies of Internet usage show that people mainly use it to maintain contact with friends and family, whom they also meet face-to-face, as well as to widen their social networks.[51] People who are active on social media tend to also be more socially active outside the Internet, have larger social networks and participate more in volunteer organizations.[52]

Social media appears to make us *more* social, not less. Generally, we have far more contact today with friends and family than we did previously.

A study of 2,000 Norwegian youths and adults over a three-year period showed that those who used social media had more acquaintances and more physical meetings, face-to-face, with their acquaintances than those who did not use social media.[53] This confirms the finding that social media does not displace other forms of sociability. Meanwhile, users of social media indicated that they were more lonely than those who did not use social media. This can of course be attributed to the idea that social media promotes loneliness, but in light of the finding that social media users are generally more social, it is more plausible to assume that this group has greater social needs and, therefore, more easily fails to have these needs met. It also appears that lonely people use the Internet more than non-lonely people.[54] Some studies, moreover, suggest that lonely people feel more lonely after using social media.[55] Nonetheless, we should not therefore assume that social media creates loneliness, because in the same period during which social media use has exploded, no evidence has emerged to suggest that loneliness itself has increased.

Indeed, this has led some people to complain that we have become too social – that loneliness is no longer accessible to us and that we are forced to live our lives in chronic social contact with others.[56] The sociologist Dalton Conley goes further and argues that the individual is being replaced by the 'intravidual'. The intravidual is a figure whose self is permeated by the social network.[57] Obviously, that seems to be an exaggeration, but the point is that most people are not more socially isolated than before: in contrast, we have become hypersocial. The loneliness problem for the liberal individual, therefore, is not an excess of loneliness, but perhaps that solitude has become too scarce, simply because the individual is so sociable.

SEVEN

Solitude

If when my wife is sleeping
and the baby and Kathleen
are sleeping
and the sun is a flame-white disc
in silken mists
above shining trees, –
if I in my north room
dance naked, grotesquely
before my mirror
waving my shirt round my head
and singing softly to myself:
'I am lonely, lonely.
I was born to be lonely,
I am best so!'
If I admire my arms, my face,
my shoulders, flanks, buttocks
against the yellow drawn shades –

Who shall say I am not
the happy genius of my household?

WILLIAM CARLOS WILLIAMS,
'Danse Russe'

Until now this book has largely been devoted to loneliness, which we would prefer to avoid because it is painful, but there is also another form of loneliness, a positive form, that we willingly seek out because it adds value to our lives. Most descriptions of loneliness are laments, but we also find praises to the phenomenon among a host of poets and philosophers. Of course, it is solitude, not loneliness, they are praising. Loneliness is more unambiguously defined than solitude. Deficiency lies at the root of loneliness, whereas solitude is more an indefinite openness to a variety of experiences, thoughts and emotions. Loneliness necessarily contains a feeling of pain or discomfort, whereas solitude does not necessarily contain any one particular emotion – often it will be experienced as positive, but it can also be emotionally neutral.

Loneliness and solitude do not necessarily exclude each other, such that those who are plagued by loneliness will automatically have no need for solitude. One can feel a definite need to be alone and still suffer from emotional or social loneliness, and one can have little need to be alone without appreciably suffering from actually being so. Those plagued by loneliness, however, do not especially tend to seek out solitude.[1]

The need to be occasionally alone seems to be a general human trait – after our childhood days are behind us, in any case. As we saw in Chapter Three, youth is a life phase characterized by a high prevalence of loneliness. Nonetheless, there is also a time when aloneness is interpreted more positively than in childhood, where the need for solitude begins to emerge. Very few seven-year-olds understand what is meant by 'solitude', whereas a majority of twelve-year-olds do.[2] In early puberty a need for more alone time arises, and the condition is willingly sought out. Indeed, those that have access to stretches of such self-chosen alone time at that age consistently prove to be better socially adapted than those who did not receive such time.[3]

In philosophy the discussion surrounding the extent to which solitude is positive can be said to have been a theme since at least antiquity. Cicero writes that man is a creature created for community with others. Solitude conflicts with human nature.[4] Devoting oneself to a solitary search for truth before the duties one has to community, not mention upholding society, is, according to Cicero, outright immoral.[5]

The first person to have devised a systematic distinction between loneliness and solitude is probably Johann Georg Zimmermann in his 1,600-page work *Solitude* (1784–5). Solitude and loneliness originate from positive and negative causes respectively. Among the negative causes, Zimmermann emphasizes idleness, misanthropy, ennui and especially 'hypochondria', which at that time was essentially synonymous with melancholy. He is also critical of hermits' and monks' 'reveries'. Such loneliness creates misanthropy and despondence. Solitude, however, creates freedom and independence, peace in which to work and a good character, and uplifts the soul. Zimmermann underscores, however, that solitude must be combined with human interaction. Indeed, Zimmermann basically attempts to find a kind of intermediary position from which to safeguard insights from both solitude's friends and foes, because 'true wisdom lies between the world and solitude'.[6] It must be said, however, that Zimmermann's analysis is much more a defence of solitude than of community. It is solitude that shows a person 'his true needs'.[7] Community, for its part, is mostly regarded as a social space for diversion and gossip.[8] Solitude harbours true recognition and true life, whereas society is a sphere of falsehood.

Christian Garve also attempts to give a balanced presentation in his two-volume work *Über Gesellschaft und Einsamkeit* (On Society and Solitude, 1979–1800), but he mostly falls on the side of society's importance.[9] Of course, Garve also emphasizes that solitude supplies the freedom and the possibility to devote oneself to something.[10] He writes that all great philosophers and poetic geniuses have loved solitude.[11] Meanwhile, solitude is downright dangerous for weak and mediocre souls because it creates melancholy, and that is linked to a state of sickness. Therefore even great philosophers and poets should seek solitude only occasionally.[12] For Garve society is the rule, and solitude the exception.

Kant, for his part, distinguishes between inferior and admirable reasons for wanting to be alone:

> We must, however, remark that *separation from all society* is regarded as sublime, if it rests upon Ideas that overlook all sensible interest. To be sufficient for oneself, and consequently to have no need of society, without at the same time being unsociable, *i.e.* without flying from it, is something bordering on the sublime; as is any dispensing with wants. On the other hand, to fly from men from *misanthropy*, because we bear ill-will to them, or from *anthropophoby* (shyness), because we fear them as foes, is partly hateful, partly contemptible. There is indeed a misanthropy (very improperly so-called), the tendency to which frequently appears with old age in many right-thinking men; which is philanthropic enough as far as *goodwill* to men is concerned, but which through long and sad experience is far removed from *satisfaction* with men. Evidence of this is afforded by the propensity to solitude . . .[13]

Kant otherwise warns against a learned philosopher eating alone, as he will lose his vivacity and mental gaiety, exhausting his thoughts and, furthermore, allowing him to miss out on those thoughts he could have enjoyed in conversation with others.[14] Placing such stress on the idea that a philosopher should seek out society is rather atypical. As we shall see, it is more common to consider solitude a prerequisite for philosophical discernment.

Solitude and Discernment

Philosophers have often emphasized solitude as something positive, as a privileged space of reflection where one can get especially close to truth.[15] Descartes stresses how one seeks the solitude of the country, away from the city and everyone familiar, in order to truly devote oneself to thinking.[16] He also mentions in many letters how much he loves solitude.

Aristotle argues that the best of all lives is the contemplative life, and that is a life that can be lived in solitude. All other virtues must be practised together with others, but the wise man is more independent than others and can therefore carry out his work alone. 'Maybe he can do it better with collaborators, but he is nevertheless the most self-sufficient.'[17] The contemplative life *can* be lived in solitude, but it does not have to be.

In the Middle Ages, solitude was generally thematized within a religious context, as a space where one had particular opportunity to approach God.[18] There is little reflection on solitude as a *problem*. Or rather, solitude is a problem to the extent that it lacks a relationship to God.[19] In solitude, in the emotion of abandonment, one feels so spiritually battered that one reopens oneself to God.

In the Renaissance there was a widespread perception that the educated must carry out their pursuits in solitude. Petrarch is probably the first person to have written an entire book on solitude: *De vita solitaria* (1346–56).[20] The work opens with Petrarch observing that all people of intellect must seek solitude by withdrawing far from cities and the people in them. Solitude provides freedom from others' demands and enables one to choose a way of life. However, one must have books for companionship: 'And indeed isolation without literature is exile, prison, and torture.'[21] Solitude alone cannot guarantee the desired tranquillity, however, since it also requires a clear mind. Petrarch further emphasizes that solitude is compatible with friendship, and that he would rather lack solitude than lack a friend.

According to Michel de Montaigne, when it comes to solitude, 'the end, I take it, is all one, to live at more leisure and at one's ease.'[22] He says that solitude can essentially be obtained anywhere, in the middle of cities or courts, but it is best to be alone. He also believes that solitude better suits old age than youth, and that one deserves to live the latter part of one's life for oneself after having lived so much for others.[23] At the same time, he stresses that this condition demands something, because we must order ourselves such that 'our content may depend wholly upon ourselves.'[24] A person, furthermore, should not spend his time on pursuits with an eye towards glory or fame, because then one is still attached to something outside oneself.

> You are no more to concern yourself how the world talks of you, but how you are to talk to yourself. Retire into yourself, but first prepare yourself there to receive yourself: it were a folly to trust yourself in your own hands, if you cannot govern yourself. A man may miscarry alone as well as in company.[25]

One must attempt to collect one's emotions and thoughts.[26]

For Ralph Waldo Emerson, it is only in solitude that a person can know himself, and even then it is not enough simply to withdraw from other people's society: one must also renounce reading and writing and be alone with the stars.[27] Emerson regards solitude as something that is both unavoidable and something to be actively pursued. He points out that one certainly needs other people, but that our meetings with them are always fleeting. Their touches are brief and pointed, as he expresses it.[28] And so one always returns to solitude, and it is solitude, not togetherness with others, that opens a way forward. Wordsworth is thinking along the same lines when he writes about the blessings of solitude after having been parted from our 'better selves' by a 'hurrying world'.[29]

Arthur Schopenhauer argues that one can only be oneself and only be free to the extent that one is solitary.[30] Therefore young people should be taught to endure solitude.[31] Essentially, a person can only be in harmony with him- or herself and never with others, not even with friends or life partners, since dissonances will always emerge in the relationship between different individuals.[32] Nonetheless, we seem to have a significant need for human attachment. Schopenhauer believes that this need essentially applies only to people of lower intellect, and that there is an inverse relationship between a person's intellectual value and his craving for others' society.[33] This craving for society, furthermore, cannot be considered innate, but is simply the result of one's inability to endure solitude.[34] The fear of solitude is more basic than our love of other people, and that fear must be overcome if one is to succeed in living a happy life.

Friedrich Nietzsche has a similar perspective. Solitude is often described as a 'home' in his writings. The wilderness metaphor also appears frequently, and it is the wilderness that enables the kind of self-collection one loses when one lives as a part of society.

> When I am among the many I live as the many do, and I do not think as I really think; after a time it always seems as though they want to banish me from myself and rob me of my soul.[35]

It is only by leaving the community and pursuing solitude that one is capable of discovering 'the higher self'. According to Nietzsche, interacting with others can be good every once in a while, but mainly so that one can then return, in relief, to solitude's embrace.[36] Nietzsche's solo-dweller regards another person, even a friend, as a hindrance to the conversation that is carried on with the self: 'For the solitary the friend is always the third one: the third one is the cork that prevents the conversation of the two from sinking into the depths.'[37] Solitude is a 'virtue' that demonstrates 'a sublime inclination to cleanliness', rather than allowing oneself to be besmirched by human society.[38] There is a good and bad solitude, however, and one may choose 'the *good* solitude, the free, high-spirited, light-hearted solitude'.[39] Nonetheless, the ability to tolerate solitude must be learned.[40] And not everyone will be capable of finding the good solitude. 'In solitude there grows whatever one brings to it, the inner beast as well. For this reason is solitude inadvisable for many.'[41] One should not, in any case, give oneself over to solitude too early – one should only do it after one has succeeded in developing character.[42] On the other hand, Nietzsche seems to think that it is only in solitude that one has the possibility of developing true character.

Surprisingly enough, solitude remains an undeveloped theme in Martin Heidegger's philosophy. As far as I can tell, the expression does not appear in *Being in Time* (1927), but the phenomenon is briefly addressed in his lectures from 1929–30, and appears in isolated places in his later writings. Still, we find no overall discussion of solitude in his works. One main problem with Heidegger's philosophy is that the 'I' has a tendency to hide from itself by erecting a kind of wall of 'self-evidence' against itself.[43] The goal is to make the self transparent in order to grasp an authentic life.[44] Our being is always a being-with, and being-with others is just as intrinsic as being-in-the-world.[45] That is the reason solitude can exist. If others were not already a part of my existence, solitude would not be a problem, because it would not exist. Being-with is wholly compatible with not being with others – it is wholly compatible with being a hermit – but even a hermit cannot avoid the thought that he is a self in a world with other selves.[46] However, Heidegger also has a tendency to emphasize that being left to oneself is actually the most innate condition. Every single one of us is predetermined to die.[47] Our being is a being-until-death. Death is a negation of who you are, but it is also that towards which you are always moving. Death individualizes. It is I myself who will die. No one can die my death for me, as they might do some other job for me, such as doing the cleaning or making a meal. Death is *my* death, a *moribundus sum* that reveals itself to us as anxiety.[48] Because death as such belongs to you alone, anxiety individualizes you and draws you back into yourself. According to Heidegger, however, this withdrawal is also a condition where the bonds to all other people are torn asunder, and such tearing is a prerequisite for living in freedom, truth and actuality.[49] Heidegger argues that our concrete being-with becomes irrelevant in this condition.[50] He uses the expression 'existential solipsism', that is, that in an existential sense one's I is the only thing that exists.[51] In that state, you are thrown entirely back on yourself, and all ties to others are cut. When you enter into truth and freedom, then, it is a freedom and truth without ties to others. That is the background for Heidegger's assertions that philosophical discernment requires solitude. Solitude can essentially be regarded as a kind of degenerate phenomenon for Heidegger, since being alone is described as an inferior mode of being with others, but for Heidegger solitude is simultaneously a prerequisite for an authentic life. Therefore it is also a prerequisite for an authentic community. For example, he writes that there are certain things that prove determinate for a community, but which cannot grow within a community – just in the individual's solitude.[52] For Heidegger, the way to self-knowledge passes through solitude. He writes that in solitude people come close to the essential in all things, close to the world and close to the self.[53] It is only in solitude that you can become who you are. And all true philosophy takes place in 'enigmatic solitude'.[54]

The thought that solitude serves as a prerequisite for insight and an authentic life can also be found in Daniel Defoe's famous novel *Robinson Crusoe* (1719), which is a moral story of solitude's purifying force. Robinson is basically a tradesman who is corrupted by his time and his own depraved nature. Isolated on an island, he comes to regret his sinful life and establishes a new relationship to God. Ultimately, he proves himself a good Christian by also converting the heathen Friday to Christianity. It is only then, after he has become a new and better person, that he can return to society. Whatever one might think of this moral fable, it is clear that solitude has a double nature that can both break a person down and facilitate a new and better relationship to oneself and others.

Rousseau and Solitude's Disappointment

Solitude is not necessarily open to those who seek it. One example of this is Jean-Jacques Rousseau. His book *Reveries of the Solitary Walker* (1776–8) provides at first glance a positive picture of solitude, but upon closer consideration proves to hold a great deal of ambivalence. Rousseau's text is peculiar, since it holds countless passages detailing how wonderful he finds his solitude, while at the same time it is obvious that between the lines – and sometimes explicitly stated – the exact opposite is the case.[55] Rousseau regards himself as a persecuted, solitary genius. The first walk sets the tone:

> I am now alone on earth, no longer having any brother, neighbor, friend, or society other than myself. The most sociable and the most loving of humans has been proscribed from society by a unanimous agreement. In the refinements of their hatred, they have sought the torment which would be cruelest to my sensitive soul and have violently broken all the ties which attached me to them.[56]

Rousseau's text, we find, is largely devoted to paranoid fantasies about his enemy's malicious conspiracies against him.

Indeed, on Rousseau's 'solitary' walks, other people are so chronically present in his mind that his walks almost lose their solitary character. In Rousseau's life, solitude was a persistent fact. Many of the character traits that we see to be particularly widespread among the lonely – such as mistrust, selfishness, a negative attitude towards others, an idea of oneself as being completely different from others, and so on – find their extreme expression in him. He made friends, but succeeded without exception in destroying these friendships. It is difficult to avoid describing Rousseau as an arsehole, but he himself says: 'but as for evil, my will has never in my life entertained it, and I doubt that there is any man in the world who has really done less of it than I.'[57]

In Rousseau's philosophy, solitude is both man's beginning and man's end. It is solitude that prevails in the natural state, where men are free, equal, self-sufficient and without prejudices. 'Natural man is entirely for himself. He is numerical unity, the absolute whole which is relative only to itself or its kind.'[58] Natural man is solitary, wild, happy and good.[59] As Kant will later observe, Rousseau's description of the natural state is so rosy that it is something of a mystery why the condition was ever left.[60] For his part, Rousseau gives no answer other than a reference to 'the work of chance',[61] as well as some general references to natural circumstances.[62] Solitude prevails in the natural state, and it is a good solitude. Civilized man, in contrast, is unhappy and immoral, has been ruined by civilization and has lost the good solitude. The goal of human life, therefore, is to regain such solitude, because only then can man be truly happy.

The norm for human life was established in Rousseau's works before the experience of solitude described in *Reveries of a Solitary Walker*, and one might assume that what is described there is the epitome of earthly delight, but such is not the case. Particularly the fifth, but also the second and seventh of his 'walks' present solitude positively, but something sorrowful, weighty and despairing hangs over the whole text. Solitude, however, is also presented as a safe haven, and especially the first and eighth walks emphasize the idea that in solitude no one can wound him. Solitude is described as a condition where one is entirely present in the moment, thereby achieving an almost mystical unity and harmony with the earth. In that state one is divinely self-sufficient. Rousseau, however, never succeeded in remaining in solitude, repeatedly returning to the society of which he never actually felt a part, always with new conflicts that seem basically to have proved his spiritual fuel. In the same way that one might wonder why man left the natural state if it was so fantastic, one might question why Rousseau always left solitude if it was so amazing. Rousseau conjures a picture of an ideal solitude, but actual solitude was always a disappointment.

Solitude's Accessibility

Very few people have lived in complete isolation from others. Most hermits lived in a community. They withdrew from large communities and built smaller communities on society's edge, usually in extremely remote places. One of modern literature's most famous independent dwellers, Henry David Thoreau, certainly did not live without social interaction for the two years, 1845–7, that he spent at Walden Pond. In spite of everything, he was only a thirty-minute walk from the town of Concord, where he gladly stopped by the tavern and visited family and friends. He does not conceal the fact that his aloneness was of a limited variety, however, and describes how nice it was to stroll into Concord every other day at least and hear the latest gossip. Many people also came to visit, not least his mother, who usually brought him a home-cooked meal. Therefore it is not all that impressive when Thoreau writes that he loves to be alone, and that he can imagine no better society than solitude.[63] Thoreau's solitude was such that it could always be abandoned at will. It was, however, another experience for Edward Abbey, who describes how as a young man he worked in a national park where people seldom appeared, and how strong his reaction was at being so alone, leading him to realize that the only thing better than being alone is being with others.[64]

Thoreau's goal is the freedom to be found in solitude. Freedom for Thoreau is the ability to do as he pleases, and solitude promotes this freedom because it both removes distractions and prevents others from placing demands on you. However, this can be achieved as well in a large city as alone in nature. Thoreau acknowledges this, and says that people who think are always solitary, and that solitude cannot be measured by the physical distance between one person and another.[65] Like loneliness, solitude can occur while one is surrounded by others, but it requires an individual to mentally sequester himself from those around him.

You can always be physically surrounded by other people, but also be in a state of solitude where you do not engage with them because you are daydreaming, have sunk into thought or are concentrating deeply on a task. In the introduction to this book, I referred to various authors' descriptions of aloneness in metropolises where a person can feel unspeakably lonely while surrounded by a crowd. Large cities, however, also provide an opportunity to seek solitude. In large cities, that is, you can enjoy a type of solitude that requires anonymity, which is more difficult to achieve in smaller locales, where the chances are greater that you will meet an acquaintance who breaks into your solitude. Therefore, it is important, for example, not to visit the same café every day, because the employees will quickly recognize you and perhaps anticipate your order – most of us, after all, are creatures of habit – and then the desired anonymity begins to dwindle because the café's employees or other regular guests nod to you and give the impression they know you, despite the fact they do not actually know anything of importance about you at all.

Private life is a kind of institutionalized version of solitude, a space where you are secured the capacity to withdraw. The fact that solitude is almost unobtainable in totalitarian societies is due to the fact that private life has been all but abolished there. Totalitarian societies are organized such that there is simply no space for private life to unfold. Indeed, such societies engender the highest conceivable levels of loneliness. Solitude is a freedom space, and establishing a private sphere is key to securing such freedom. As Friedrich Hayek writes: 'Freedom thus presupposes that the individual has some assured private sphere, that there is some set of circumstances in his environment with which others cannot interfere.'[66] The concept of 'private' varies with time and place, and private life has its own history.[67] Nonetheless, it appears that every culture has some concept of private life.[68] Freedom must be the freedom to live one's life in one's *own* way. This presupposes a private life, because private life constitutes a sphere where the 'own' can be shaped. Basically, private life forms an independent space where one can devote oneself to oneself, where one can reflect on oneself, where one can forget oneself or play out sides of the self that otherwise would not come to expression, and in some cases, should not come to expression beyond that sphere. Certain aspects of life can only exist under the presupposition that we can be entirely left to ourselves. The I in the poem 'Danse Russe' by William Carlos Williams, which appears at the beginning of this chapter, does nothing wrong when he dances, but it is not something he wishes others to see. He is showing a side of himself to himself that can only appear when he is alone. Superman's retreat is called The Fortress of Solitude, and is the only place he can truly be himself, without having to present another persona to the surrounding world. Though we may not be superheroes, the rest of us require such a space as well. As John Stuart Mill observes:

It is not good for man to be kept perforce at all times in the presence of his species. A world from which solitude is extirpated, is a very poor ideal. Solitude, in the sense of being often alone, is essential to any depth of meditation or of character; and solitude in the presence of natural beauty and grandeur, is the cradle of thoughts and aspirations which are not only good for the individual, but which society could ill do without.[69]

The place where we are most often alone is our own home.[70] Home is therefore the central place for both solitude and loneliness. When I write that solitude is solely realizable within the framework of private life, however, that does not mean that one necessarily succeeds in realizing it there. You can have a private life that contains not a shred of solitude, but in contrast is permeated by loneliness. Your private life could be characterized by such chronic engagement with others, not least through the use of social media, that neither solitude nor loneliness enters in. Private life, therefore, does not guarantee solitude – it requires instead self-effort. Conversely, one can imagine a person's private sphere to be so full to bursting with other people, especially family, who demand one's attention, that solitude is only accessible when he or she actually leaves the private sphere and enters public space.

Freedom from the Gaze of Others

Solitude does not have to unfold within a private life framework, but it is most easily realized there. The reason for this is that being the object of other people's gazes influences our relationship to ourselves.

Jean-Paul Sartre describes humans as lonely, and they must experience the pain that loneliness brings in order to recognize their place in the universe. However, human life is also always realized in togetherness with others. The interpretation here is not that a person first exists for himself and then joins others. Human existence is always necessarily a being-with. Indeed, being-with is actually a prerequisite for our getting to know ourselves. We get to know ourselves through other people's eyes. I am sitting in a park looking at everything around me. I am the centre point of all this – everything exists solely for me. I am a 'subject' and transform everything around me into an object. But suddenly another person appears in my field of view. At first I consider that person to be just another random object, but soon I discover that the person distinguishes himself from all other objects because he relates to his surroundings in the same way I do. The other is also a subject and, accordingly, he does not just see all the things that I see, but he can also see me. The other person transforms me into an object for him. It is only now that he actually becomes a fellow human being for me, since I am required to recognize him as a subject. Furthermore, it is also only now that I can achieve a true relation to myself. The experience of being seen enables me to see myself. For example, take a case where you are standing outside a door, eavesdropping. All your attention is directed at what is taking place on the other side of that door. Suddenly, someone taps you on the shoulder and you blush because you have been uncovered. Only then do you become truly aware of yourself as you are, namely, someone who listens at doors.[71] That is, you recognize yourself through the other person's judgement of you. The other is someone who judges you with his eyes, and that gaze penetrates your soul.[72] That experience constitutes your relationship to others: they judge you. Nonetheless, you need those others, because the acknowledgement you require must come from others, and for that acknowledgement to have any value, you must also acknowledge others. The value of others' acknowledgement of me depends on my acknowledgement of them.[73]

At the same time, I require a relationship to myself that is not defined by the gaze of others, where I do not have the external relationship to myself that emerges because I observe myself in order to ensure that I appear to others as I want to appear. In solitude I achieve a more direct relationship to myself because it is not mediated by others' gaze. In solitude we escape the experience of being an object for another person. This constitutes a freedom from others. When you are alone, you therefore have the opportunity to escape relating to yourself in such a reflexive way. It appears that people are less self-conscious when they are alone.[74] When people seek solitude, it is to achieve not only freedom *from* others, but *to* decide for themselves what to do and what to think about.[75] That does not mean that one must be uncompromisingly self-absorbed in that condition. Much that we do in solitude has a purpose that extends beyond that solitude.

In the first lecture of *Some Lectures Concerning the Scholar's Vocation* (1794), Johann Gottlieb Fichte emphasizes that the scholar is first and foremost a person, and as a person he is a social being. Therefore, the scholar will live in opposition to his nature if he isolates himself and chooses solitude.[76] In *The System of Ethics* (1798), Fichte stresses that even though solitary contemplation can be beneficial for a thinker, the goal of that contemplation presupposes communication with other people.[77]

Most people who write books can only do that when they are alone, in solitude. Marguerite Duras emphasizes this idea in *Writing*:

> The solitude of writing is a solitude without which writing could not be produced, or would crumble, drained bloodless by the search for something else to write . . . The person who writes books must always be enveloped by a separation from others. That is one kind of solitude. It is the solitude of the author, of writing.[78]

However, the goal of solitary writing is that one's writing will find a reader. Even though an important reason for my writing is that others will read what I have written, I am nonetheless not capable of writing if someone is peeking over my shoulder while I do it. At that point, I become too self-conscious and am unable to be present in what I am writing. Much of the time we spend in solitude concerns our relationship to others, about how we can best exist in the world with them. Even though we choose solitude, we are still social creatures.

The Solitude Capability

In Chapter Three, we discussed some tests for loneliness. There is also a test for solitude, the Preference for Solitude Scale (1995). The significant increase in the number of people who choose to live and go on holiday alone suggests that more people today have a preference for solitude, but I have not found a single study that has measured this phenomenon over time. We can additionally remark that the frequency of and pleasure in being alone most strongly correlate to the individual enjoying the condition in and of itself, and not simply wishing to avoid social contact.[79] Even while people are largely choosing to live and holiday alone, however, they seem to be less alone than ever, simply because they are in chronic interaction with others, not least via the electronic communication devices they always carry with them.

We live in a time when most of us are hardly ever left to ourselves, where telephone conversations, text messages, Twitter, Facebook and Skype ensure that we are chronically interacting with others. Access to solitude is scarcer then it was before, in particular because we have chosen to fill the space where solitude could have existed with sociality. Perhaps our era's greatest problem then is not excessive loneliness, but rather too little solitude. Solitude is threatened when we – be it from boredom, restlessness, uncertainty or laziness – grasp too quickly for others, either face-to-face or via the telephone or computer, rather than remain in our solitary condition. We let ourselves be seized by, or we reach too easily for, distractions. The word is interesting: dis-traction, literally 'being drawn apart'. What are drawn apart from is ourselves.

Bertrand Russell argued in 1937 that we had lost solitude.[80] Similarly, Odo Marquard asserts that we have largely lost 'the solitude capability'.[81] However, aside from the obvious point that it concerns our capacity to be alone, what does 'solitude capability' imply? Marquard writes: 'Maturity is above all the capacity for solitariness.'[82] This is a rather strange assertion, to be sure, but the point here is that maturity requires that a person be capable of standing alone with his convictions without leaning on others for support. According to Kant, enlightenment signifies man's overcoming just such immaturity.[83] Of course, it must be added that Kant is writing about intellectual immaturity, whereas the incapacity to establish solitude speaks more of emotional immaturity. The difficulty with solitude is that one is forced to relate to oneself, and to succeed in finding peace within this self-relationship. Lacking such peace, we seek distraction, which can draw us away from ourselves. As Pascal writes:

> We do not seek that easy and peaceful lot which permits us to think of our unhappy condition, nor the dangers of war, nor the labour of office, but the bustle which averts these thoughts of ours, and amuses us.
>
> Reasons why we like the chase better than the quarry.
>
> Hence it comes that men so much love noise and stir; hence it comes that the prison is so horrible a punishment; hence it comes that the pleasure in solitude is a thing incomprehensible.[84]

The chronic need for distraction is a sign of emotional immaturity. Apparently, such immaturity is typical. In studies where people are left entirely to their thoughts for as little as six to fifteen minutes, a majority of subjects report having medium or above difficulty with the task.[85] When subjects are given the opportunity to 'cheat', by playing with their phones, for example, a majority do just that. One study allowed subjects to break the monotony by delivering a painful electric shock to themselves, and a quarter of the women and two-thirds of the men did just that. Indeed, one person shocked himself 190 times in fifteen minutes. These studies are as much tests of the capacity to endure boredom as they are studies of solitude, but they do reveal an incapacity for many people to fill oneself with oneself when external distractions are removed.

As Nietzsche writes: 'I have gradually seen the light as to the most universal deficiency in our kind of cultivation and education: no one learns, no one strives after, no one teaches – *the endurance of solitude*.'[86] The solitude capability is something that must be learned. Thomas Macho writes about what he calls 'solitude techniques', that is, techniques that enable one to be in society with oneself.[87] In loneliness, one is alone with oneself, whereas in solitude, one is together with oneself. A general characteristic of these techniques is that they imply a self-doubling, where you do not create an exact copy of yourself, but rather another self with whom to converse. In other words, you successfully allow yourself to be filled with your own presence rather than the absence of others. Samuel Butler describes the melancholic as someone who has landed in the world's worst society: his own.[88] The society Butler describes is so dreadful because it essentially involves an absence, a loss, a lack.

The lack of some kind of rich, inner life makes it hard to abandon oneself to solitude. On the other hand, solitude as such seems to be a prerequisite for having a rich, inner life. Mihaly Csikszentmihalyi found that people who have difficulty tolerating aloneness, who have difficulty finding solitude, also have considerable difficulty developing themselves creatively. Only those who master the technique of aloneness seem to succeed in art or science.[89] Of course, these people are also in constant interaction with others. What characterizes creative people is not that they are more solitary than others, but rather that they are capable of using their solitude to create something rather than simply despairing at the condition.[90]

Hannah Arendt points out that loneliness is a fundamental experience in every human life and also in conflict with our most basic needs.[91] For Arendt, philosophy is a solitary activity. She describes 'the philosopher' who leaves 'the dark cave of human affairs'[92] for solitude. And, as Arendt notes, 'to be in solitude means to be with one's self.'[93] This phenomenon, however, is not simply reserved for those who are called philosophers. All solitude, according to Arendt, is distinguished by the fact that I am together with myself: I am 'two-in-one'.[94] Of course, solitude can transform into loneliness, and Arendt suggests that when this happens I am abandoned by myself. That is, when I do not succeed in dividing myself into 'two-in-one', and remain alone without the society of myself.[95]

The difference between solitude and loneliness particularly consists in the relationship one has to oneself in that condition, if one succeeds in remaining relatively self-sufficient. Of course, no one is entirely self-sufficient, which itself would hardly be ideal, but without a certain amount of self-sufficiency, without the capacity to be present in oneself without leaning on others for support, a person will lead a rather miserable life. After all, one cannot always be leaning on others. Self-sufficiency is never total, however, and in order for solitude to be positive, a way back to other people must exist. As Olav H. Hauge writes:

It is sweet, solitude,
as long as the way back
to others
remains open.
After all, you don't shine
for yourself.[96]

EIGHT

Loneliness and Responsibility

They always say time changes things, but you actually have
to change them yourself.

ANDY WARHOL, *The Philosophy of Andy Warhol*
(From A to B and Back Again)

There is little reason to believe that loneliness is a growing
problem in the late modern world, but it does represent a
substantial problem. Even for those of us not severely affected
by loneliness, it is still an important phenomenon, because
it reveals how much we actually need other people in our
lives. And a not insignificant minority of us are more or less
chronically relegated to this painful emotion.[1]

Loneliness and Shame

Why is loneliness so painful? Loneliness tells us something
about ourselves, about our place in the world. The emotion
tells us how insignificant we are in the greater scheme of
things. We feel relegated to a universe where we make no difference, where our being or non-being is devoid of relevance
for our surroundings. Loneliness is particularly tied to shame.

Sometimes when I have given lectures on loneliness, I
have asked the lonely in the audience to raise their hands, but
no hand appears and an uncomfortable silence sets in. This
idea illustrates a point: the difficulty people have in publicly

admitting to loneliness. Loneliness, after all, is a social pain, an ache that signals that one's social life is not satisfactory, and that pain becomes especially discomfiting when it becomes socially visible. Loneliness is not only painful, but embarrassing. In order to avoid the shame, it is essential a person maintain the impression of having a thriving social life, however lonely that person might feel. Despite the fact that loneliness is a general human phenomenon, whoever suffers from loneliness is a loser.

In Joan Didion's *Play It as It Lays*, we follow the 31-year-old actress Maria Wyeth's path to a mental institution, from her divorce from her husband, the abortion he forced her to have, a daughter's hospitalization and a career in free-fall. Maria is deeply lonely, and it is critical for her to hide this loneliness:

> She had watched them in supermarkets and she knew the signs. At seven o' clock on a Saturday evening they would be standing in the checkout line reading the horoscope in *Harper's Bazaar* and in their carts would be a single lamb chop and maybe two cans of cat food and the Sunday morning paper, the early edition with the comics wrapped outside. They would be the very pretty some of the time, their skirts the right length and their sunglasses the right tint and maybe only a little vulnerable tightness around the mouth, but there they were, one lamb chop and some cat food and the morning paper. To avoid giving off the signs, Maria shopped always for a household, gallons of grapefruit juice, quarts of green chile salsa, dried lentils and alphabet noodles, rigatoni and canned yams, twenty-pound boxes of laundry detergent. She knew all the indices to the idle lonely, never bought a small tube of toothpaste, never dropped a magazine in her shopping cart. The house in Beverly

Hills overflowed with sugar, corn-muffin mix, frozen roasts and Spanish onions. Maria ate cottage cheese.[2]

To be lonely is to fail at an essential part of human life, because it means failing to form the needed relationships to one or more people. The lonely do not receive acknowledgment of their human worth from others, at least not to the extent they require. Therefore loneliness appears to be imposed on the individual from without. The lonely person is someone who desires, but lacks, a relationship to other people. There is a difference, however, between being socially withdrawn and socially excluded.

Loneliness, Belonging and Life Meaning

Chronic loneliness and experimentally imposed social isolation are correlated with lower levels of experienced life meaning. This suggests that belonging is essential in order for us to experience our lives as meaningful.[3] Life meaning can of course be studied from a variety of different perspectives, but one consistent trait appears to be that a person's relationship to others plays a decisive role.[4] There is good evidence to support Baumeister and Leary's 'belonging hypothesis' which states, 'human beings have a pervasive drive to form and maintain at least a minimum quantity of lasting, positive, and impactful interpersonal relationships.'[5] However, it must be added that not everyone has the same need for belonging, that is, some people exhibit this to a greater or lesser extent.[6] People who spend much of their time with others are typically happier than those who spend much of their time alone, but obviously there is substantial individual variation. In measurements of subjective well-being – or 'happiness', as it is often misleadingly termed – interpersonal relationships make a greater impact than money and health. If you want to try and predict whether a person will score high or low on a scale of subjective well-being, the time the individual in question spends together with family and friends would give you among the best odds for guessing correctly. People report to a large extent that they experience more positive feelings when they are together with others than when they are alone. That being said, most people can also have a wonderful time in their own society and a terrible time in others'.

Nonetheless, the truth is that we all need other people. And a key factor in this need for others is a need to be needed by others. In a certain sense, those who are not needed by others play no role. Therefore, it is strange that we largely organize our lives around needing others to the least possible degree. In 1970 the sociologist Philip Slater published the book *The Pursuit of Loneliness*, where he wrote:

> We seek a private house, a private means of transportation, a private garden, a private laundry, self-service stores, and do-it-yourself skills of every kind. An enormous technology seems to have set itself the task of making it unnecessary for one human being ever to ask anything of another in the course of going about his or her daily business. Even within the family Americans are unique in their feeling that each member should have a separate room, and even a separate telephone, television, and car, when economically possible. We seek more and more privacy, and feel more and more alienated when we get it.[7]

In a sense, the decades that have passed since Slater published his book have only strengthened this development towards increasingly greater independence. Hegel would have that this is a description of the miserable self that 'cannot renounce his isolation and withdrawal into himself or tear himself free from this unsatisfied abstract inwardness'.[8] However, there is little to suggest that we have become any lonelier.

Responsibility for Your Own Emotions

The phenomenology of loneliness is such that loneliness appears imposed from without. That one's environment is to blame. And if one's environment is to blame, it follows that it is left to one's environment to remediate the situation. However, we must all take responsibility for our own emotions. Your emotions *are* your emotions. They belong to you. Aristotle argues that no person can avoid acting according to his character, but that such actions are also in a certain sense voluntary, because we have generated our own character, that is, we have partially created or shaped ourselves.[9] For example, you can be held responsible for cultivating a habitual anger that causes you react to certain situations with unreasonable aggression. Similarly, we can argue that an individual can be considered responsible for his own loneliness if he has chosen a behavioural pattern that maintains and strengthens that loneliness. Harry Frankfurt, for his part, explicitly rejects the Aristotelian theory, and argues instead that being responsible for one's character – and the actions it occasions – is not a question of producing or shaping that character, but rather of 'taking responsibility for it'.[10] Meanwhile, it seems clear that a person can bear such responsibility only to the extent it is possible to alter said character.

Naturally, we cannot choose what to feel. You cannot simply decide not to be lonely, thereby causing the problem to vanish like dew before the sun by an act of will alone. Phenomenologically speaking, emotions are something that happen to us, and are often in direct conflict with what we might otherwise desire. However, you can also choose, for example, to enter a social situation, despite the discomfort it causes you. You can try and change the way you think about such situations, about the expectations you have of other people and your attachment to them. That is a task no one can do for you.

On the other hand, loneliness is experienced as being imposed from without, as resulting from an unsatisfactory social environment that does not live up to one's expectations. It might therefore seem unfair to suggest that lonely people should change their relationship to themselves and their environment. Is that not 'victim blaming'? In this case, the lonely might wish to respond as Morrissey does in The Smiths' song 'How Soon Is Now?'

> You shut your mouth
> how can you say
> I go about things the wrong way
> I am human and I need to be loved
> just like everybody else does

The pain of loneliness is the pain of insufficient acknowledgement. Complaints of loneliness are complaints of the pain caused by a basic human need going unfulfilled. That need, however, is partially a product of one's own expectations. Therefore, perhaps one should not be too quick to conclude that there is something wrong with the social support that others provide. Perhaps the problem is rather the expectations one brings to these relationships. Perhaps today we generally expect too much warmth in the social sphere.[11] If one perpetually feels lonely, even though one is surrounded by family and friends that provide typical support and acknowledgement, there is something amiss with one's 'social hunger', just as some people continue to feel hungry even though, strictly speaking, they have already overeaten. One can continually search for new romantic relationships and new friends in the hope that they can fill one's need for attachment – though that is hardly possible. In this case, loneliness comes to bear the mark of dysfunction, just as other emotions can become dysfunctional.

I cannot tell you why you are lonely, if in fact you are. I have discussed some of the social circumstances and psychological characteristics that increase a person's chance of experiencing loneliness, but it is up to you to determine the relevance this discussion has for you, in terms of the causes and basis of your particular loneliness. Perhaps some of the material presented in this book can also function as a corrective for your self-understanding. Perhaps you will find that the causes and basis for your loneliness are not what you thought they were. Loneliness is experienced as being externally imposed, because one's environment is inadequate to meet one's emotional need for attachment, but perhaps you will also realize that you possess some character traits that help to shape that perception, such as your expectations for actual attachment being too great, or that you are not sufficiently trusting, that you are too self-absorbed, or that you are too critical of yourself and others in social situations.

In many cases, it will be correct to say: you are not lonely because you are alone – you are alone because you are lonely. As mentioned, such a statement could be perceived as unjust to the lonely, and as a version of victim blaming. Despite everything, loneliness does feel as though it is externally imposed by an environment that is inadequate to one's needs. This subjective idea, however, is not a good indicator of the causes of loneliness. If you are surrounded by supportive family and friends, and nonetheless continue to feel lonely, it is tempting to say that your need for acknowledgement has run awry. The fact that you are lonely does not necessarily mean that others have failed you or that they have fallen short. It can be that it is you who have fallen short in your evaluation of the attachment you actually have to them. Your loneliness, furthermore, does not mean you can expect others to remedy that loneliness. No one has a right to a life without loneliness, just as no one has a right to be happy.

A gap will always exist between the way you experience yourself and the way others experience you, and you are conscious of this difference. You are present in your own thoughts and experiences in a way that no other person can ever be. Therein dwells loneliness, a kind most people handle just fine most of the time, but one that can also become burdensome. From that perspective, the paradigmatic loneliness experience is not located in other's absence, but in the presence of others from whom one feels distant. Our need for friendship and love is an expression of the need to overcome this alienation, to be tied to other people who, at least partway, can say that they understand what you think and can feel what you feel, and not just because you have stated what you think and feel, but because they really know you. These others do not necessarily need to applaud your thoughts and emotions, but to understand where these thoughts and emotions come from and to recognize them as an expression of who you are and how you experience the world. It involves a special form of immediacy between two people, which is the closest we can come to bridging the loneliness to which we are all basically relegated for our entire lives.

At the same time, there is so much we cannot share. Death is lonely. Your death is precisely that: your death. Pascal writes: 'We are fools to depend upon the society of our fellow-men. Wretched as we are, powerless as we are, they will not aid us; we shall die alone.'[12] Norbert Elias also writes about 'the loneliness of dying' and argues that death in our culture is hidden rather than emerging as a part of our world experience. As such, death is problematic for the living, and that leads to loneliness among the dying 'if – still living – they are made to feel that [they] are already excluded from the community of the living'.[13] However, it does not have to be that way. It does not need to be like 'The Death Song' by Jens Bjørneboe, from the play *The Bird Lovers* (1966):

Now the day has arrived and the hour has arrived.
And you are placed against the wall to bleed.
And the ones who hold you dear

Soon fade away from you
That's when you will see: it is lonesome to die.[14]

Those who care about you will not necessarily fade away.
When my father died, we were with him throughout the entire
process. We knew what was going to happen, and spent many
late nights talking about it. None of us could die for him, but
we were there with him. There was a closeness and comfort
right up until the end, as a continuation of everything we had
previously had together. Nonetheless, it was a fact for him that
it was he who was going to die.

It is Your Loneliness

Loneliness tells me something about myself, about my place
in the world. In younger and dumber days, I believed I did
not necessarily need others, that I could be self-sufficient.
Occasionally, I can still be seduced by the positive emotion
of solitude into thinking that self-sufficiency is still an alter-
native. The illusion never persists for long, and solitude is
replaced by loneliness. That sense of loneliness reveals significant limits for who we can be, simply because it so decisively
shows us that we are not self-sufficient. From the time we are
born, from before we are born, our lives are woven together
with others and throughout our lives new ties are formed
while old ties are torn asunder. As D. H. Lawrence observes,
human life is such that everything in it, even our individuality,
depends on our relationship to others.[15] Without such relationships, the majority of our individuality would evaporate,
precisely because it is something that is developed and defined
through our relation to others.

As Richard Ford's novel *Canada* puts it:

Loneliness, I've read, is like being in a long line,
waiting to reach the front where it's promised

something good will happen. Only the line never moves, and other people are always coming in ahead of you, and the front, the place where you want to be, is always farther and farther away until you no longer believe it has anything to offer you.[16]

However, it is mistaken to believe that ultimately this queue – life – has nothing to offer. Others can recognize your loneliness only to the extent that you show it. No one else can force their way into your loneliness and compel it to vanish. However, you can allow someone into your loneliness, and at that point it is no longer a loneliness, but a community. Then you must learn to live with the fact that every human life will contain loneliness to some degree. This is why it is so critical to learn to tolerate loneliness and to hopefully transform that loneliness into solitude.

Loneliness can be reduced by learning to rest in yourself, so that you are not so dependent on others' acknowledgement of you, while at the same time seeking others out and opening yourself to them. Still, loneliness will inevitably strike from time to time. It is a loneliness for which you must take responsibility. For despite everything, it is *your* loneliness.

References

Introduction

1 Stendhal, *On Love*, p. 267.
2 C. S. Lewis, *The Four Loves*, p. 12.
3 Simmel, 'The Metropolis and Mental Life', p. 108. See also Simmel, *Sociology: Inquiries into the Construction of Social Forms*, p. 95.
4 Simmel, *The Philosophy of Money*, p. 298.
5 Tocqueville, *Democracy in America*, pp. 665, 701.
6 Tocqueville, *Selected Letters on Politics and Society*, p. 326. On solitude in the wilderness, see further Tocqueville, 'Journey to Lake Oneida' and 'A Fortnight in the Wilderness', p. 665.
7 Cf. Marquard, 'Plädoyer für die Einsamkeitsfähigkeit', p. 113; Moody, 'Internet Use and its Relationship to Loneliness'; Monbiot, 'The Age of Loneliness is Killing Us'.
8 Chen and French, 'Children's Social Competence in Cultural Contexts'.
9 Cf. Svendsen, *Philosophy of Boredom*, p. 28.
10 Larson, 'The Solitary Side of Life: An Examination of the Time People Spend Alone from Childhood to Old Age'.
11 Cioran, *Drawn and Quartered*, p. 159.
12 Sartre, *Nausea*, p. 116.
13 Rilke, *Letters to a Young Poet*, p. 23.
14 Genesis 2:18.
15 Psalms 142:4.
16 Ecclesiastes 4:9–12.
17 Kant, *Idea of a Universal History with a Cosmopolitan Purpose*, p. 44.
18 Byron, *Childe Harold's Pilgrimage*, Canto III, v. 90, p. 131.

19 Milton, Paradise Lose, Book IX, 249, p. 192.

20 Bierce, *The Enlarged Devil's Dictionary*, p. 44.

21 Butler, 'A Melancholy Man', p. 59.

22 MacDonald and Leary, 'Why Does Social Exclusion Hurt? The Relationship Between Social and Physical Pain'; Eisenberger, Lieberman and Williams, 'Does Rejection Hurt? An fMRI Study of Social Exclusion'.

23 A good, precise overview of the genetic and neuroscientific aspects of loneliness can be found in Hawkley and Cacioppo, 'Perceived Social Isolation: Social Threat Vigilance and its Implication for Health'. There is an extensive psychoanalytic literature on loneliness that I will take up only in limited capacity. For an overview and discussion of many of the most central contributions, see Quindoz, *The Taming of Solitude: Separation Anxiety in Psychoanalysis*.

ONE The Essence of Loneliness

1 For example, the Norwegian Institute of Public Health gives this definition of loneliness: 'Good social support means that one receives love and care, is respected and valued, and that one belongs to a social network and a community with mutual responsibilities. The opposite of good social support is loneliness.' Folkehelseinstituttet, 'Sosial støtte og ensomhet – faktaark'.

2 Cf. Scarry, *The Body in Pain*.

3 Eliot, *The Cocktail Party*, p. 414.

4 An extreme expression of such metaphysical loneliness is Ben Lazare Mijuskovic's *Loneliness in Philosophy, Psychology and Literature* (1979), which reduces the entirety of human existence to a state of loneliness, and where those who might claim that loneliness is not so defining of his or her life cannot be described in any other way than individuals living in denial of their basic existential condition. Interpersonal communication is dismissed as a momentary, albeit comforting, illusion (Mijuskovic, *Loneliness in Philosophy, Psychology and Literature*, p. 82). Mijuskovic claims that loneliness is the most fundamental fact of human life, that loneliness is the basic structure of self-consciousness, and that when one attempts to see through themselves completely, they find an emptiness

or desolation, in short: loneliness (ibid., pp. 13, 20). However, one can question whether this type of Cartesian introspection, where the self is made utterly transparent to itself, is even possible. Many philosophers, not least Kant, have provided arguments for why this is more than doubtful. One can further question why such introspection should yield a more basic truth than that revealed by extrospection. However that may be, the most important thing to keep in mind is that reflections such as Mijuskovic's are so reductive and general that they overlook all multiplicity in the phenomenon they have set out to examine. It is tempting to turn to a Shakespearean citation that Wittgenstein considered using as a motto for *Philosophical Investigations*, 'I'll teach you differences!' (Shakespeare, *King Lear*, Act I, Scene 4.) As Wittgenstein underscored in his remarks to Frazer's *The Golden Bough*: 'Nothing is so difficult as doing justice to the facts.' (Wittgenstein, *Philosophical Occasions, 1912–1951*, p. 129.) It is the craving for generality that complicates matters (Wittgenstein, *The Blue Book*, pp. 17f). Indeed, Mujuskovic appears to be someone who, suffering from chronic loneliness, generalizes from his own experiences when he writes that a person can momentarily overcome the emotion of loneliness, but that such relief is never permanent or even particularly long-lasting (Mijuskovic, *Loneliness in Philosophy, Psychology and Literature*, p. 9). Most people, however, do not experience loneliness as Mijuskovic describes it. Of course, he can certainly try to contend that most people live in some sort of denial of their basic existential condition, but it is difficult to regard the arguments he provides for this as especially compelling.

5   Russell, *Autobiography*, p. 160, cf. p. 137.
6   Kahneman et al., 'A Survey Method for Characterizing Daily Life Experience: The Day Reconstruction Method'; Emler, 'Gossip, Reputation and Social Adaptation'.
7   Cacioppo, Hawkley and Berntson, 'The Anatomy of Loneliness'; Wheeler, Reis and Nezlek, 'Loneliness, Social Interaction, and Sex Roles'; Hawkley et al., 'Loneliness in Everyday Life: Cardiovascular Activity, Psychosocial Context, and Health Behaviors'.
8   Sermat, 'Some Situational and Personality Correlates of Loneliness', p. 308.

9 Cacioppo and Patrick, *Loneliness*, p. 94.

10 See especially Peplau and Perlman, 'Perspectives on Loneliness'; Perlman and Peplau, 'Toward a Social Psychology of Loneliness'.

11 Cf. Russell et al., 'Is Loneliness the Same as Being Alone?'

12 Tilburg, "The Size of Supportive Network in Association with the Degree of Loneliness'.

13 See for example Reis, 'The Role of Intimacy in Interpersonal Relations'.

14 Cf. Hawkley and Cacioppo, 'Loneliness Matters: A Theoretical and Empirical Review of Consequences and Mechanisms'.

15 Stillman et al., 'Alone and Without Purpose: Life Loses Meaning Following Social Exclusion'; Williams, 'Ostracism: The Impact of Being Rendered Meaningless'.

16 Baumeister and Vohs, 'The Pursuit of Meaningfulness in Life'; Heine, Proulx and Vohs, 'The Meaning Maintenance Model: On the Coherence of Social Motivations'.

17 James, *The Principles of Psychology*, vol. I, pp. 293–4.

18 Dostoyevsky, *Notes from the Underground*, p. 33.

19 Kierkegaard, *Sickness Unto Death*, p. 43.

20 Smith, *Theory of Moral Sentiments*, p. 84.

21 Ibid., p. 110.

22 Ibid., p. 153.

23 Shaftesbury, *Characteristics of Men, Manners, Opinions, Times*, p. 215.

24 Burke, *Philosophical Inquiry into the Origin of our Ideas of the Sublime and the Beautiful*, p. 53.

25 Locke, *Two Treatises of Government*, p. 318.

26 Locke, *Of the Conduct of the Understanding*, §45, p. 285.

27 Hume, *A Treatise on Human Nature*, Book II.ii.v, p. 363.

28 Hume, *Inquiries Concerning Human Understanding and Concerning the Principles of Morals*, p. 270.

29 See for example Cacioppo and Patrick, *Loneliness*.

30 Cf. Long and Averill, 'Solitude: An Exploration of Benefits of Being Alone', p. 38.

31 Bowlby, *Attachment and Loss*, vol. III: *Loss: Sadness and Depression*, p. 442.

32 Cf. Young, 'Loneliness, Depression, and Cognitive Therapy: Theory and Application'.

33 Barthes, *Mourning Diary*, p. 69.

34 Murakami, *Colorless: Tsukuru Tazaki and His Years of Pilgrimage*.

35 Mahon and Yarcheski, 'Loneliness in Early Adolescents:
    An Empirical Test of Alternate Explanations'; Mahon and
    Yarcheski, 'Alternate Explanations of Loneliness in Adolescents:
    A Replication and Extension Study'.

36 Weiss, *Loneliness: The Experience of Emotional and Social
    Isolation*.

37 Another difference between these types of loneliness is that
    anxiety has a stronger correlation to social loneliness than
    emotional loneliness. (DiTommaso and Spinner, 'Social and
    Emotional Loneliness: A Re-examination of Weiss' Typology
    of Loneliness'.)

38 Weiss, *Loneliness*, p. 48.

39 Cf. Victor and Yang, 'The Prevalence of Loneliness Among
    Adults: A Case Study of the United Kingdom'.

40 Geller et al., 'Loneliness as a Predictor of Hospital Emergency
    Department Use'.

41 Holt-Lunstad, Smith and Layton, 'Social Relationships and
    Mortality Risk: A Meta-Analytic Review'. See further Cacioppo
    and Cacioppo, 'Social Relationships and Health: The Toxic
    Effects of Perceived Social Isolation'.

42 For a good overview of somatic correlates regarding loneliness,
    see Cacioppo and Patrick, *Loneliness*, ch. 6.

43 Hawkley and Cacioppo, 'Aging and Loneliness – Downhill
    Quickly?'

44 Hawkley and Cacioppo, 'Perceived Social Isolation: Social
    Threat Vigilance and its Implication for Health', pp. 770–71.

45 Cacioppo and Patrick, *Loneliness*, p. 99.

46 For discussions of loneliness in the context of different
    psychiatric diagnoses, see for example Coplan and Bowker,
    eds, *The Handbook of Solitude: Psychological Perspectives on
    Social Isolation, Social Withdrawal, and Being Alone.*

47 Cacioppo, Hawkley and Thisted, 'Perceived Social Isolation
    Makes Me Sad: 5-Year Cross-lagged Analyses of Loneliness
    and Depressive Symptomatology in the Chicago Health,
    Aging, and Social Relations Study'.

48 Stravynski and Boyer, 'Loneliness in Relation to Suicide Ideation
    and Parasuicide: A Population-wide Study'; Rojas, *Childhood
    Social Exclusion and Suicidal Behavior in Adolescence and Young
    Adulthood.*

49 Baumeister, Twenge and Nuss, 'Effects of Social Exclusion

on Cognitive Processes: Anticipated Aloneness Reduces Intelligent Thought'; Baumeister et al., 'Social Exclusion Impairs Selfregulation'; Twenge et al., 'If You Can't Join Them, Beat Them: Effects of Social Exclusion on Aggressive Behavior'; Twenge, Catanese and Baumeister, 'Social Exclusion Causes Self-defeating Behavior'; Twenge, Catanese and Baumeister, 'Social Exclusion and the Deconstructed State: Time Perception, Meaninglessness Lethargy, Lack of Emotion, and Self-awareness'; Twenge et al., 'Social Exclusion Decreases Prosocial Behavior'.
50 Cf. Ozcelic and Barsade, 'Work Loneliness and Employee Performance'.

TWO Loneliness as Emotion

1 Ben-Ze'ev, *The Subtlety of Emotions*, p. 5.
2 Ibid., p. 470.
3 Eisenberger, Lieberman and Williams, 'Does Rejection Hurt? An fMRI Study of Social Exclusion'.
4 MacDonald and Leary, 'Why Does Social Exclusion Hurt? The Relationship Between Social and Physical Pain'.
5 Cf. Lieberman, *Social: Why Our Brains are Wired to Connect*, pp. 64ff.
6 Here I will especially emphasize Ben-Ze'ev, *The Subtlety of Emotions*.
7 Ekma, 'An Argument for Basic Emotions'; Solomon, 'Back to Basics: On the Very Idea of "Basic Emotions"'.
8 Cf. Ortony et al., *The Cognitive Structure of the Emotions*, p. 27.
9 For a good discussion that takes such an approach, see Gross, *The Secret History of Emotion: From Aristotle's Rhetoric to Modern Brain Science*.
10 Asher and Paquette, 'Loneliness and Peer Relations in Childhood'.
11 Taylor, *Philosophical Papers*, vol. I: *Human Agency and Language*, p. 63.
12 Aristotle, *Nicomachean Ethics*, 1094b24.
13 La Rochefoucauld, *Collected Maxims*, §27.
14 Heidegger, *Nietzsche*, p. 99.
15 Ibid., p. 51.
16 Heidegger, *Hölderlin's Hymns 'Germania' and 'The Rhein'*.

17 Heidegger, *Pathmarks*, p. 87.
18 Heidegger, *History of the Concept of Time: Prologmena*, p. 296.
19 Beckett, *Dream of Fair to Middling Women*, p. 6.
20 Heidegger, *The Fundamental Concepts of Metaphysics: World, Finitude, Solitude*, p. 6.
21 Ibid., p. 67.
22 Wittgenstein, *Tractatus logico-philosophicus*, §6.43.
23 Cf. Hawkley et al., 'Loneliness in Everyday Life: Cardiovascular Activity, Psychosocial Context, and Health Behaviors'.
24 Aristotle, *Rhetoric*, 1382a.
25 Aristotle, *Nicomachean Ethics*, 1115b.
26 Shaver, Furman and Buhrmester, 'Transition to College: Network Changes, Social Skills, and Loneliness'.
27 Flett, Hewitt and Rosa, 'Dimensions of Perfectionism, Psychosocial Adjustment, and Social Skills'.
28 Heidegger, *Being and Time*, p. 148.
29 Heidegger, *Hölderlin's Hymns*, p. 89.
30 Heidegger, *Being and Time*, p. 136.
31 Heidegger, *Hölderlin's Hymns*, p. 142.

THREE Who are the Lonely?

1 Victor et al., 'Has Loneliness amongst Older People Increased? An Investigation into Variations between Cohorts'; Victor, Scrambler and Bond, *The Social World of Older People*.
2 Cf. AARP, *Loneliness among Older Adults: A National Survey of Adults 45+*.
3 The data used here is taken from the survey 'Samordnet levekårsundersøkelse 1980–2012'. Statistics Norway (SSB) is responsible for the collection of the data. The data is assembled and made available in anonymized form by Norwegian Social Science Data Services (NDS). Neither SSB nor NDS is responsible for the analysis of the date or the interpretations made here. A huge thanks to Thomas Sevenius Nilsen at the Norwegian Institute for Public Health for help with processing the figures.
4 For an overview of a portion of these studies, see Yang and Victor, 'Age and Loneliness in 25 European Nations'; Victor and Yang, 'The Prevalence of Loneliness Among Adults: A Case Study of the United Kingdom'.

5　See, for example, Pinquart and Sorensen, 'Influences on Loneliness in Older Adults: A Meta-analysis'. On the other hand,
there are also studies that conclude that loneliness levels are
lower in old age, but that deviates from most other studies (cf.
Gibson, *Loneliness in Later Life*).

6　Rotenberg, 'Parental Antecedents of Children's Loneliness'.

7　Cacioppo and Patrick, *Loneliness*, p. 24; Cacioppo, Cacioppo
and Boomsma, 'Evolutionary Mechanisms for Loneliness';
Goossens et al., 'The Genetics of Loneliness: Linking
Evolutionary Theory to Genome-wide Genetics, Epigenetics,
and Social Science'; Distel et al., 'Familiar Resemblance for
Loneliness'.

8　Lucht et al., 'Associations between the Oxytocin Receptorgene
(OXTR) and Affect, Loneliness and Intelligence in Normal
Subjects'.

9　Cf. Norman et al., 'Oxytocin Increases Autonomic Cardiac
Control: Moderation by Loneliness'.

10　Halvorsen, *Ensomhet og sosial isolasjon i vår tid*, p. 84, 110.

11　Tornstam, 'Loneliness in Marriage'.

12　Yang and Victor, 'Age and Loneliness in 25 European Nations'.

13　Ibid.

14　An exception to this is that men who live alone more often
report a significant feelings of loneliness than women who live
alone. (Olds and Schwartz, *The Lonely American*, p. 82).

15　See, for example, Pinquart and Sorensen, 'Influences on Loneliness in Older Adults: A Meta-analysis'.

16　See, for example, Borys and Perlman, 'Gender Differences in
Loneliness'.

17　Yang and Victor, 'Age and Loneliness in 25 European Nations'.

18　Olds and Schwartz, *The Lonely American*, p. 117.

19　Knut Halvorsen utilizes both explanations in his loneliness
study, where first he indicates that the difference is alone due to
the fact that women are more open about their loneliness than
men. However, when he discusses loneliness among disabled
boys and girls, he opens the possibility that the difference can
be due to the fact that girls have different expectations of loneliness than boys. (Halvorsen, *Ensomhet og sosial isolasjon i vår
tid*, pp. 114, 117.)

20　Boomsma et al., 'Genetic and Environmental Contributions to
Loneliness in Adults: The Netherlands Twin Register Study'.

21 Cf. Baumeister, *The Cultural Animal: Human Nature, Meaning, and Social Life*, p. 111.

22 Tornstam, 'Loneliness in Marriage'.

23 Vanhalst et al., 'The Development of Loneliness from Mid- to Late Adolescence: Trajectory Classes, Personality Traits, and Psychosocial Functioning'.

24 Cacioppo and Patrick, *Loneliness*, p. 94.

25 Ibid., p. 30.

26 Ibid., pp. 13–14. See also Bell and Daly, 'Some Communicator Correlates of Loneliness'; Wanzer, Booth-Butterfield and Booth-Butterfield, 'Are Funny People Popular? An Examination of Humor Orientation, Loneliness, and Social Attraction'.

27 Teppers et al., 'Personality Traits, Loneliness, and Attitudes toward Aloneness in Adolescence'; Cacioppo et al., 'Loneliness within a Nomological Net: An Evolutionary Perspective'.

28 Duck, Pond and Leatham, 'Loneliness and the Evaluation of Relational Events'. See also Jones, 'Loneliness and Social Contact'; Jones and Moore, 'Loneliness and Social Support'; Jones, Sanson, and Helm, 'Loneliness and Interpersonal Judgments'; Spitzberg and Canary, 'Loneliness and Relationally Competent Communication'.

29 Cf. Jones, Freemon and Goswick, 'The Persistence of Loneliness: Self and Other Determinants'.

30 Bellow, *Herzog*.

31 Kupersmidt et al., 'Social Self-discrepancy Theory and Loneliness During Childhood and Adolescence'.

32 Lau and Gruen, 'The Social Stigma of Loneliness: Effect of Target Person's and Perceiver's Sex'; Rotenberg and Kmill, 'Perception of Lonely and Non-lonely Persons as a Function of Individual Differences in Loneliness'.

33 Cf. Hawkley et al., 'Loneliness in Everyday Life: Cardiovascular Activity, Psychosocial Context, and Health Behaviors'.

34 Ernst and Cacioppo, 'Lonely Hearts: Psychological Perspectives on Loneliness'; Vaux, 'Social and Emotional Loneliness: The Role of Social and Personal Characteristics'.

35 Cacioppo and Patrick, *Loneliness*, p. 103.

36 Cf. Twenge et al., 'Social Exclusion Decreases Prosocial Behavior'.

37 DeWall and Baumeister, 'Alone but Feeling no Pain: Effects of Social Exclusion on Physical Pain Tolerance and Pain Threshold, Affective Forecasting, and Interpersonal Empathy'.

38 Jones, Hobbs and Hockenbury, 'Loneliness and Social Skill Deficits'.

39 Bell, 'Conversational Involvement and Loneliness'.

40 Solano, Batten and Parish, 'Loneliness and Patterns of Self-disclosure'.

41 Goswick and Jones, 'Loneliness, Self-concept, and Adjustment'.

42 Lemay and Clark, '"Walking on Eggshells": How Expressing Relationship Insecurities Perpetuates Them'.

43 Bell, 'Emotional Loneliness and the Perceived Similarity of One's Ideas and Interests'.

44 Weisbuch and Ambady, 'Affective Divergence: Automatic Responses to Others' Emotions Depend on Group Membership'.

45 Cf. Twenge and Campbell, *The Narcissism Epidemic*, pp. 191–2.

46 Shaver, Furman and Buhrmester, 'Transition to College: Network Changes, Social Skills, and Loneliness'.

47 Cacioppo and Patrick, *Loneliness*, p. 163.

48 Flett, Hewitt and Rosa, 'Dimensions of Perfectionism, Psychosocial Adjustment, and Social Skills'.

49 Næss, *Bare et menneske*, p. 37.

50 Ibid., p. 7.

51 Ibid., p. 213.

52 Ibid., p. 36.

53 Ibid., p. 132.

54 Ibid., p. 250.

55 Gardner et al., 'On the Outside Looking In: Loneliness and Social Monitoring'.

56 Dandeneau et al., 'Cutting Stress Off at the Pass: Reducing Vigilance and Responsiveness to Social Threat by Manipulating Attention'; Murray et al., 'Balancing Connectedness and Self-protection Goals in Close Relationships: A Levels-of-Processing Perspective on Risk Regulation'.

57 DeWall et al., 'It's the Thought that Counts: The Role of Hostile Cognition in Shaping Aggressive Responses to Social Exclusion'.

58 Maner et al., 'Does Social Exclusion Motivate Interpersonal Reconnection? Resolving the "Porcupine Problem"'.

FOUR Loneliness and Trust

1 It must be observed that at present too little research has been conducted to clarify the relationship between these phenomena. In loneliness research, there are just a handful of studies that take up the connection, and in trust research loneliness remains largely un-themed. See the following studies: Rotenberg, 'Loneliness and Interpersonal Trust'; Rotenberg et al., 'The Relationship between Loneliness and Interpersonal Trust during Middle Childhood'; Rotenberg et al., 'The Relation Between Trust Beliefs and Loneliness during Early Childhood, Middle Childhood, and Adulthood'.

2 Rotenberg et al., 'The Relation between Trust Beliefs and Loneliness during Early Childhood, Middle Childhood, and Adulthood'.

3 Halvorsen, *Ensomhet og sosial isolasjon i vår tid*, p. 75.

4 Auster, *The Invention of Solitude*, p. 50.

5 Cf. 'Loneliness in Everyday Life: Cardiovascular Activity, Psychosocial Context, and Health Behaviors'.

6 Ernst and Cacioppo, 'Lonely Hearts: Psychological Perspectives on Loneliness', and Vaux, 'Social and Emotional Loneliness: The Role of Social and Personal Characteristics'.

7 Bell, 'Emotional Loneliness and the Perceived Similarity of One's Ideas and Interests'.

8 Simmel, *The Philosophy of Money*, p. 191.

9 For measurements of trust levels in different countries and its development over time, see www.worldvaluessurvey.org/wvs.jsp.

10 OECD, 'Trust', in Society at a Glance, 2011: OECD Social Indicators, pp. 90–91.

11 Such an assumption is supported by Chen, 'Loneliness and Social Support of Older People in China: a Systematic Literature Review'. However, it must be observed that this study demonstrates great variation among different surveys. See further Wang et al., 'Loneliness among the Rural Older People in Anhui, China: Prevalence and Associated Factors', and Yang and Victor, 'The Prevalence of and Risk Factors for Loneliness among Older People in China'.

12 See for example, OECD, Society at a Glance, 2014: OECD Social Indicators, pp. 138ff.

13 Wollebæk and Segaard, *Sosial kapital i Norge*.

14 A common suggestion has been that ethnic homogeneity creates trust and ethnic diversity reduces trust, but this appears to only partially be the case. In neighbourhoods with greater ethnic diversity, there is a lower level of trust between neighbours, but this ethnic diversity does not appear to create lower levels of generalized trust. (Cf. Meer and Tolsma, 'Ethnic Diversity and its Effects on Social Cohesion'.)

15 Cf. Fukuyama, *Political Order and Political Decay*, pp. 97–125, see especially pp. 123ff.

16 Bergh and Bjørnskov, 'Historical Trust Levels Predict the Current Size of the Welfare State'.

17 Arendt, *The Origins of Totalitarianism*, p. 478.

18 Ibid., p. 477.

19 Cf. Hosking, *Trust: A History*, ch. 1.

20 See, for example, Schlögel, *Moscow, 1937*, p. 194.

21 Arendt, *The Origins of Totalitarianism*, p. 323.

22 Arendt, *Denktagebuch 1950 bis 1973. Erster Band*, pp. 126–7. Thanks to Helgard Mahrdt for drawing my attention to this citation.

23 Arendt, *The Human Condition*, p. 59.

24 Aristotle, *Nicomachean Ethics*, 1161b9.

25 Eliot, *Middlemarch*, p. 273.

26 Cf. Grimen, *Hva er tillit*, p. 109.

27 La Rochefoucauld, *Collected Maxims*, §84.

28 Ibid., §86.

29 Fukuyama, *Trust: The Social Virtues and the Creation of Prosperity*, pp. 27, 152–3.

30 Løgstrup, *The Ethical Demand*, p. 8.

31 Cf. Hawkley et al., 'Loneliness in Everyday Life: Cardiovascular Activity, Psychosocial Context, and Health Behaviors'.

32 Rotenberg et al., 'The Relation between Trust Beliefs and Loneliness during Early Childhood, Middle Childhood, and Adulthood'.

33 Terrell, Terrell and von Drashek, 'Loneliness and Fear of Intimacy among Adolescents who were Taught Not to Trust Strangers during Childhood'.

34 Shallcross and Simpson, 'Trust and Responsiveness in Strain-test Situations: A Dyadic Perspective'.

FIVE Loneliness, Friendship and Love

1 See for example Caine, ed., *Friendship: A History*, and May, *Love: A History*.
2 Aristotle, *Politics*, 1253a.
3 Ibid.
4 Aristotle, *Nicomachean Ethics*, 1169b10.
5 Ibid., 1156a9.
6 Ibid., 1156b7–12.
7 Ibid., 1156b25.
8 Ibid., 1166a30.
9 Kant, *Lectures on Ethics*, pp. 24, 27, 54.
10 Kant, *The Metaphysics of Morals*, pp. 216–17.
11 Ibid., p. 217.
12 Kant, *Lectures on Ethics*, pp. 185–6.
13 Ibid., p. 410.
14 Ibid., p. 25.
15 Ibid., p. 182.
16 Ibid., pp. 413–14.
17 Kant, 'On the Character of the Species', in *Anthropology from a Pragmatic Point of View*, Part II.E, p. 184.
18 Ibid., part II.E, p. 190. On this, see further Kant, *Lectures on Anthropology*, pp. 499–500.
19 Kant, 'Idea for a Universal History with a Cosmopolitan Purpose', p. 44. See also *Metaphysics of Morals*, p. 216.
20 On this subject, see further Kant, *Lectures on Ethics*, p. 174.
21 Kant, *Metaphysics of Morals*, pp. 216–17.
22 Ibid., p. 216.
23 Kant, *Lectures on Ethics*, p. 190.
24 See especially Montaigne, 'Of Solitude'.
25 Montaigne, 'Of Friendship', p. 383.
26 Ibid., pp. 390–91.
27 Ibid., pp. 391, 393.
28 Ibid., p. 397.
29 Ibid., p. 400.
30 Cf. Aristotle, *Rhetoric*, 1380b36.
31 Simmel, *Sociology*, p. 321.
32 Plato, *Symposium*, 189d–190a.
33 Ibid., 191a–b.
34 Ibid., 193c.
35 *Abelard and Heloise: The Letters and Other Writings.*

36 Goethe, *The Sorrows of Young Werther*, p. 25.
37 Ibid., p. 31.
38 Ibid., p. 86.
39 Ibid., p. 53.
40 Ibid., p. 127.
41 Heidegger, *History of the Concept of Time: Prolomegna*, pp. 296–7.
42 Milligan, *Love*, p. 3.
43 Cited from Arkins, *Builders of My Soul: Greek and Roman Themes in Yeats*, p. 148.
44 Joyce, 'A Portrait of the Artist as a Young Man' and 'Dubliners', p. 409. The example is taken from Milligan, *Love*, pp. 16–17.
45 Baudelaire, *Paris Spleen*, pp. 51–2.
46 Mykle, *Largo*, p. 114.
47 Tolstoy, *Family Happiness and Other Stories*, p. 38.
48 Frankfurt, *The Importance of What We Care About*, p. 170.
49 Jaspers, 'The Individual and Solitude', p. 189.
50 Ibid.
51 Jaspers, *Philosophie II. Existenzerhellung*, p. 61.
52 Ibid., p. 62.
53 Rilke, *Letter to a Young Poet*, p. 35.

six Individualism and Loneliness

1 Beck and Beck-Gernsheim, *Individualization: Institutionalized Individualism and its Social and Political Consequences*, p. xxii.
2 Beck, *Risk Society*, p. 122.
3 Mill, *Principles of Political Economy with Some of their Applications to Social Philosophy*, p. 938.
4 See especially Berlin, *Liberty*. I have analysed the concepts of negative and positive freedom in *The Philosophy of Freedom*, ch. 6.
5 Sen, *Rationality and Freedom*, chs 20–22.
6 See especially Simmel, 'Die beiden Formen des Individualismus', and Simmel, 'Kant und der Individualismus'.
7 Simmel, *Kant. Die Probleme der Geschichtsphilosophie*, p. 220.
8 Simmel, 'Die beiden Formen des Individualismus', p. 54. In and of itself, this is no unreasonable assertion, but it is rather surprising that Simmel does not one mention that the most radical variant of Romantic, liberal individualism is developed

by Wilhelm von Humboldt in *The Limits of State Action* (1792), which in its own right proved a main source of inspiration for John Stuart Mill's liberalism, where the necessity of an individual space for the development of a unique personality was central to political philosophy and social philosophy.

9   Simmel, 'The Metropolis and Mental Life'.
10 Cf. Giddens, *Modernity and Self-identity: Self and Identity in the Late Modern Age*, p. 5, and Giddens, *The Transformations of Intimacy*, p. 30.
11 Nietzsche, *The Gay Science*, §270, cf. §335.
12 Dostoyevsky, *Notes from the Underground*.
13 Cf. Taylor, *The Ethics of Authenticity*, p. 40.
14 Mead, *Mind, Self and Society*.
15 Sandel, *Liberalism and the Limits of Justice*, p. 179.
16 Cf. Marar, *The Happiness Paradox*.
17 Cf. Klinenberg, *Going Solo*, p. 3.
18 Ibid., pp. 4–5.
19 Olds and Schwartz, *The Lonely American*, p. 82.
20 EU, *Independent Living for the Ageing Society*.
21 Klinenberg, *Going Solo*, p. 160.
22 Ibid., p. 10.
23 Schumpeter, *Capitalism, Socialism and Democracy*, pp. 157–8.
24 Gerstel and Sarkisian, 'Marriage: The Good, the Bad, and the Greedy'; Musick and Bumpass, 'Reexamining the Case for Marriage: Union Formation and Changes in Well-being'. See also Klinenberg, *Going Solo*.
25 DePaulo, 'Single in a Society Preoccupied with Couples'.
26 Mellor et al., 'Need for Belonging, Relationship Satisfaction, Loneliness, and Life Satisfaction'.
27 Klinenberg, *Going Solo*, pp. 98ff.
28 Marche, 'Is Facebook Making Us Lonely?'.
29 Weber, *The Protestant Ethic and the Spirit of Capitalism*, p. 60.
30 Tocqueville, *Democracy in America*, p. 884.
31 Fukuyama, 'The Great Disruption', *Atlantic Monthly*.
32 Putnam, *Bowling Alone*, p. 158.
33 For a good overview, see Thompson, 'The Theory that Won't Die: From Mass Society to the Decline of Social Capital', p. 423.
34 Ibid., p. 425.
35 Putnam, *Bowling Alone*, p. 403.
36 Fischer, *Still Connected: Family and Friends in America since*

1970. See also Fischer, *Made in America: A Social History of American Culture and Character*.

37 Fischer, *Made in America*, p. 155.

38 McPherson, Smith-Lovin and Brashears, 'Social Isolation in America: Changes in Core Discussion Networks over Two Decades'.

39 Fischer, 'The 2004 Finding of Shrunken Social Networks: An Artifact'.

40 Rokach et al., 'The Effects of Culture on the Meaning of Loneliness'; Rokach, 'The Effect of Age and Culture on the Causes of Loneliness'.

41 Lykes and Kemmelmeier, 'What Predicts Loneliness? Cultural Difference Between Individualistic and Collectivistic Societies in Europe'.

42 De Jong Gierveld and Van Tilburg, 'The De Jong Gierveld Short Scales for Emotional and Social Loneliness: Tested on Data from Seven Countries in the UN Generations and Gender Surveys'.

43 Lykes and Kemmelmeier, 'What Predicts Loneliness? Cultural Difference Between Individualistic and Collectivistic Societies in Europe'.

44 Diener and Diener, 'Cross-cultural Correlates of Life Satisfaction and Self-esteem'.

45 Cf. Beck and Beck-Gernsheim, *Individualization*, p. xxii.

46 Dreyfus, *On the Internet*.

47 Turkle, *Alone Together*.

48 Kraut et al., 'Internet Paradox. A Social Technology that Reduces Social Involvement and Psychological Well-being'.

49 Kraut et al., 'Internet Paradox Revisited'.

50 Whitty and McLaughlin, 'Online Recreation: The Relationship between Loneliness, Internet Self-efficacy and the Use of the Internet for Entertainment Purposes'.

51 Cf. Rainie and Wellman, *Networked: The New Social Operating System*.

52 Hampton et al., *Social Isolation and New Technology*.

53 Brandtzæg, 'Social Networking Sites: Their Users and Social Implications – A Longitudinal Study'.

54 Amichai-Hamburger and Schneider, 'Loneliness and Internet Use'.

55 Ibid.

56 Deresiewicz, 'The End of Solitude'.

57 Conley, *Elsewhere, U.S.A.*, p. 104.

SEVEN Solitude

1   Cf. Long and Averill, 'Solitude: An Exploration of Benefits of Being Alone'.

2   Galanaki, 'Are Children Able to Distinguish among the Concepts of Aloneness, Loneliness, and Solitude?'

3   Larson, 'The Emergence of Solitude as a Constructive Domain of Experience in Early Adolescence'.

4   Cicero, *On Friendship*, p. 83.

5   Cicero, *On Duties*, Book I, ch. 43ff.

6   Zimmermann, *On Solitude*, vol. IV, pp. 373–4.

7   Ibid., vol. I, p. 286.

8   Ibid., vol. I, pp. 20, 29–30.

9   Garve, *Über Gesellschaft und Einsamkeit*.

10 Ibid., vol. I, pp. 55–6.

11 Ibid., vol. I, p. 99.

12 Ibid., vol. I, p. 334.

13 Kant, *Critique of Judgement*, p. 87.

14 Kant, *Anthropology from a Pragmatic Point of View*, Part I, §88, pp. 143–4.

15 This is not just true of philosophy. In the Bible God has a tendency to impart His message to people when they are alone. Moses received the Torah after spending forty days alone on Mount Sinai. Paul was alone when he received his revelation on the way to Damascus. Even though Jesus was undoubtedly a social figure, he often withdrew to pray in solitude, and he ordered his disciples to do the same. Early saints went out in the wilderness, away from their fellow men, to experience the tests Jesus had undergone there, and through this isolation to achieve a closer bond with God. Muhammad received his first revelation when he was alone in his cave on Jabal al-Nour. Ultimately, revelations seem to take place in solitude.

16 Descartes, *A Discourse on the Method of Correctly Conducting One's Reason and Seeking Truth in the Sciences*, p. 27.

17 Aristotle, *Nicomachean Ethics*, 1177a–b.

18 See for example Eckhart, 'On Detachment'.

19 Cf. St John of the Cross, *Dark Night of the Soul*, chs VI–VII, pp. 52–7.

20 Petrarch, *The Life of Solitude*.

21 Ibid., p. 131.

22 Montaigne, 'Of Solitude', p. 481.

23 Ibid., pp. 488–9.

24 Ibid., p. 485.

25 Ibid., p. 498.

26 Cf. Montaigne, 'Of Three Commerces', pp. 1220–21.

27 Emerson, 'Nature'.

28 Emerson, 'Experience', p. 322.

29 Wordsworth, *The Prelude*, Book 4, ll. 354–8, p. 161.

30 Schopenhauer, *Parerga and Paralipomena*, I, p. 24.

31 Ibid., p. 26.

32 Ibid.

33 Ibid., pp. 28–9.

34 Ibid., p. 27.

35 Nietzsche, *Daybreak*, §491, p. 201.

36 Nietzsche, *Human, All too Human*, vol. II, §333, p. 344. Cf. Nietzsche, *Daybreak*, §566, p. 227.

37 Nietzsche, *Thus Spoke Zarathustra*, p. 49.

38 Nietzsche, *Beyond Good and Evil*, §284, p. 171.

39 Ibid., §25, p. 26.

40 Nietzsche, *Daybreak*, §443, p. 188.

41 Nietzsche, *Thus Spoke Zarathustra*, p. 255.

42 Nietzsche, *Nachgelassene Fragmente*, 1880–1882, p. 110.

43 Heidegger, *The Basic Problems of Phenomenology*, §10, p. 78.

44 Heidegger, *Plato's Sophist*, p. 36.

45 Heidegger, *Being and Time*, p. 115; Heidegger, *History of the Concept of Time: Prolegomena*, p. 238.

46 Heidegger, *Being and Time*, pp. 116–17.

47 Heidegger, *History of the Concept of Time: Prolegomena*, pp. 317–18

48 Heidegger, *Being and Time*, p. 254.

49 Ibid., p. 240.

50 Heidegger, *History of the Concept of Time: Prolegomena*, pp. 317–18.

51 Heidegger, *Being and Time*, p. 182. Cf. Heidegger, O*ntology: The Hermeneutics of Facticity*, pp. 6–7.

52 Heidegger, *Logic as the Question Concerning the Essence of Language*, p. 45.

53 Heidegger, *The Fundamental Concepts of Metaphysics: World, Finitude, Solitude*, p. 6.

54 Heidegger, *What is Called Thinking?*, p. 169.

55 Rousseau, *Reveries of the Solitary Walker*.

56 Ibid., p. 1.

57 Ibid., p. 84.

58 Rousseau, *Emile, or, On Education*, p. 39.

59 In other words, the exact opposite of Thomas Hobbes's description of human life in a natural state, 'solitary, poor, nasty, brutish, and short' (Hobbes, *Leviathan*, p. 76).

60 Kant, 'Conjectural Beginning of Human History', p. 174.

61 Rousseau, *Discourse on Inequality*, p. 41.

62 Ibid., pp. 34–5.

63 Thoreau, *Walden*, p. 131.

64 Abbey, *Desert Solitaire: A Season in the Wilderness*.

65 Thoreau, *Walden*, p. 131.

66 Hayek, *The Constitution of Liberty*, p. 61.

67 Cf. Ariès and Duby, eds, *A History of Private Life*; Weintraub and Kumar, eds, *Public and Private in Thought and Practice*.

68 Cf. Moore, Jr, *Privacy*.

69 Mill, *Principles of Political Economy*, p. 756.

70 Long and Averill, 'Solitude: An Exploration of Benefits of Being Alone', p. 30.

71 Cf. Sartre, *Being and Nothingness*, pp. 347ff.

72 Ibid., p. 321.

73 Ibid., p. 320.

74 Larson, 'The Solitary Side of Life: An Examination of the Time People Spend Alone from Childhood to Old Age'.

75 Hammitt, Backman and Davis, 'Cognitive Dimensions of Wilderness Privacy: An 18-year Trend Comparison'.

76 Fichte, 'Some Lectures Concerning the Scholar's Vocation'.

77 Fichte, *The System of Ethics*, p. 262.

78 Duras, *Writing*, p. 2.

79 Leary et al., 'Finding Pleasure in Solitary Activities: Desire for Aloneness or Disinterest in Social Contact?'

80 Russell, *Unpopular Essays*, pp. 67–8.

81 Marquard, 'Plädoyer für die Einsamkeitsfähigkeit'.

82 Ibid., p. 120. See also Marquard, Farewell to Matters of Principle, p. 16.

83 Kant, 'An Answer to the Question: What is Enlightenment?', p. 41.

84 Pascal, *Pensées*, pp. 39–40.
85 Wilson et al., 'Just Think: The Challenges of the Disengaged Mind'.
86 Nietzsche, *Daybreak*, §443, p. 188.
87 Macho, 'Mit sich allein. Einsamkeit als Kulturtechnik'. See also Sloterdijk, *You Must Change Your Life*, pp. 361ff.
88 Butler, 'A Melancholy Man', p. 59.
89 Csikszentmihalyi, *Creativity*, pp. 65–6.
90 Ibid., p. 177.
91 Arendt, *The Origins of Totalitarianism*, p. 475.
92 Arendt, *The Human Condition*, p. 226.
93 Ibid., p. 75.
94 Arendt, *The Origins of Totalitarianism*, p. 476.
95 Arendt, *The Life of the Mind,* vol. i: *Thinking*, p. 185.
96 Hauge, 'Attum einsemds berg'.

EIGHT Loneliness and Responsibility

 1 Heinrich and Gullone, 'The Clinical Significance of Loneliness: A Literature Review'.
 2 Didion, *Play It as It Lays*, pp. 122–3.
 3 Stillman et al., 'Alone and Without Purpose: Life Loses Meaning Following Social Exclusion'; Williams, 'Ostracism: The Impact of Being Rendered Meaningless'.
 4 Baumeister and Vohs, 'The Pursuit of Meaningfulness in Life'; Heine, Proulx and Vohs, 'The Meaning Maintenance Model: On the Coherence of Social Motivations'.
 5 Baumeister and Leary, 'The Need to Belong: Desire for Inter-personal Attachments as a Fundamental Human Motivation', p. 497. For an elaboration, see Baumeister, *The Cultural Animal*.
 6 Gere and MacDonald, 'An Update of the Empirical Case for the Need to Belong'; Mellor et al., 'Need for Belonging, Relationship Satisfaction, Loneliness, and Life Satisfaction'; Kelly, 'Individual Differences in Reactions to Rejection'.
 7 Slater, *The Pursuit of Loneliness*, p. 5.
 8 Hegel, 'Introduction to Aesthetics', in *Hegel's Aesthetics*, p. 66.
 9 Aristotle, *Nicomachean Ethics*, 1114b22.
10 Frankfurt, *Taking Ourselves Seriously and Getting it Right*, p. 7.
11 As Richard Sennet writes, 'The reigning belief today is that closeness between persons is a moral good. The reigning

aspiration today is to develop individual personality through experiences of closeness and warmth with others. The reigning myth today is that the evils of society can all be understood as evils of impersonality, alienation, and coldness. The sum of these three is an ideology of intimacy: social relationships of all kinds are real, believable, and authentic the closer they approach the inner psychological concerns of each person. This ideology transmutes political categories into psychological categories. The ideology of intimacy defines the humanitarian spirit of a society without gods: warmth is our god' (Sennett, *The Fall of Public Man*, p. 259).

12 Pascal, *Pensées*, pp. 61–2.
13 Elias, *The Loneliness of the Dying*, p. 66.
14 Bjørneboe, *The Bird Lovers*, p. 153.
15 Lawrence, *Late Essays and Articles*, pp. 297–8.
16 Ford, *Canada*, p. 292.

Bibliography

AARP, *Loneliness among Older Adults: A National Survey of Adults 45+*, www.aarp.org/content/dam/aarp/research/surveys_statistics/general/2012/loneliness_2010.pdf

Abbey, Edward, *Desert Solitaire: A Season in the Wilderness* [1968] (New York, 1985)

Abelard, Pierre, and Heloise, *Abelard and Heloise: The Letters and Other Writings*, trans. and intro. William Levitan (Indianapolis, IN, and Cambridge, 2007)

Amichai-Hamburger, Yair, and Barry H. Schneider, 'Loneliness and Internet Use', in *The Handbook of Solitude: Psychological Perspectives on Social Isolation, Social Withdrawal, and Being Alone*, ed. Robert J. Coplan and Julie C. Bowker (Malden, MA, and Oxford, 2014)

Arendt, Hannah, *Denktagebuch 1950 bis 1973. Erster Band* (Munich and Zürich, 2002)

——, *The Human Condition*, 2nd edn, intro. Margaret Canovan [1958] (Chicago, IL, 1998)

——, *The Life of the Mind*, vol. I: *Thinking* (San Diego, CA, New York and London, 1977)

——, *The Origins of Totalitarianism* (San Diego, CA, New York and London, 1979)

Ariès, Philippe, and Georges Duby, eds, *A History of Private Life*, 5 vols (Cambridge, MA, 1992)

Aristotle, *Nicomachean Ethics*, trans. and ed. Roger Crisp (Cambridge and New York, 2000)

——, *Rhetoric*, trans. W. Rhys Roberts, ed. W. D. Ross (New York, 2010)

——, *Politics*, 2nd edn, trans. and intro. Carnes Lord (Chicago, IL, and London, 2013)

Arkins, Brian, *Builders of My Soul: Greek and Roman Themes in Yeats* (Savage, MD, 1990)

Asher, Steven R., and Julie A. Paquette, 'Loneliness and Peer Relations in Childhood', *Current Directions in Psychological Science*, 3 (2003)

Auster, Paul, *The Invention of Solitude* (New York, 1982)

Aydinonat, Denise, et al., 'Social Isolation Shortens Telomeres in African Grey Parrots (*Psittacus erithacus erithacus*)', PLOS ONE, 9 (2014)

Barthes, Roland, *Mourning Diary*, trans. Richard Howard (New York, 2010)

Baudelaire, Charles, *Paris Spleen: Little Poems in Prose*, trans. Keith Waldrop (Middletown, CT, 2009)

Baumeister, Roy F., *The Cultural Animal: Human Nature, Meaning, and Social Life* (Oxford, 2005)

—, and Mark R. Leary, 'The Need to Belong: Desire for Inter-personal Attachments as a Fundamental Human Motivation', *Psychological Bulletin*, 3 (1995)

—, Jean M. Twenge and Christopher K. Nuss, 'Effects of Social Exclusion on Cognitive Processes: Anticipated Aloneness Reduces Intelligent Thought', *Journal of Personality and Social Psychology*, 83 (2002)

—, and Kathleen D. Vohs, 'The Pursuit of Meaningfulness in Life', in *Handbook of Positive Psychology*, ed. C. R. Snyder and Shane J. Lopez (New York, 2002)

—, et al., 'Social Exclusion Impairs Self-regulation', *Journal of Personality and Social Psychology*, 88 (2005)

Beck, Ulrich, *Risk Society Towards a New Modernity (London*, 1992)

—, and Elisabeth Beck-Gernsheim, *Individualization: Institutionalized Individualism and its Social and Political Consequences* (London, 2002)

Beckett, Samuel, *Dream of Fair to Middling Women* (Dublin, 1992)

Bell, Brad, 'Emotional Loneliness and the Perceived Similarity of One's Ideas and Interests', *Journal of Social Behavior and Personality*, 2 (1993)

Bell, Robert A., 'Conversational Involvement and Loneliness', *Communication Monographs*, 52 (1985)

—, and J. A. Daly, 'Some Communicator Correlates of Loneliness', *Southern States Communication Journal*, 2 (1985)

Bellow, Saul, *Herzog* (New York, 1964)